The Fayoum

The Fayoum

History and Guide

New Revised Edition

R. Neil Hewison

with photographs by the author

The American University in Cairo Press
Cairo • New York

The American University in Cairo Press
113 Sharia Kasr el Aini, Cairo, Egypt
420 Fifth Avenue, New York, NY 10018
www.aucpress.com

First and second editions published in 1984 and 1986 as *The Fayoum: A Practical Guide*

Dar el Kutub No. 4412/08
ISBN 978 977 416 206 0

Dar el Kutub Cataloging-in-Publication Data

Hewison, R. Neil
The Fayoum: History and Guide. New Revised Edition / R. Neil Hewison.—Cairo: The American University in Cairo Press, 2008
p. cm.
ISBN 977 416 206 4
1. El Fayoum—history I. Title
962.23

1 2 3 4 5 6 7 8 14 13 12 11 10 09 08

Designed by Andrea El-Akshar
Printed in Egypt

إلى
الحاج محمد صالح البرعصى وعائلته الكريمة بالأبعادية
الذين استقبلونى بحفاوة بالغة فى بيتهم وفى حياتهم
واعتبرونى واحداً منهم

This edition is dedicated to
Hagg Mohamed Saleh el-Barassy and his family of al-Ab‘âdiya,
who welcomed me into their house and their lives
and generously counted me as one of their own

Contents

Illustrations

Sobek, the Fayoum's ancient patron crocodile deity
Inside the Middle Kingdom temple of Qaṣr al-Ṣâgha
The Middle Kingdom pyramid of Hawwâra
The Old Kingdom pyramid of Sêla
The Middle Kingdom temple of Madînat Mâḍi
A Ptolemaic lion at Madînat Mâḍi

between pages 78 and 79

Maps

Map references in the text are given in parentheses, by map number and grid square, e.g., Sêla pyramid (1F2).

Acknowledgments

My debts of gratitude from earlier editions of this book remain: to Mr. Sabry Ghabbour, Mr. Adel Ali, Mr. Mohammed Tantawy, Mr. Ahmed Abd al-Aal, and Mr. Nabil Hanzal. For this edition, I am very grateful for the help of Mr. Ibrahim Abd al-Baset, assistant lecturer in Egyptology at the Faculty of Tourism and Hotels, Fayoum University.

A Note on Pronunciation

The system used in this book for transcribing Arabic names and words is as arbitrary as any other, so requires a little explanation, particularly for those unfamiliar with Arabic.

Consonants

For the four symbols ṣ, ḍ, ṭ, ẓ (representing ص, ض, ط, and ظ, the so-called emphatics), imagine you are going to say 'oo' (as in 'cool'), then, without moving your tongue, pronounce *s, d, t, z.* Your tongue should be bunched up in the back of your mouth.

ḥ represents the sound ح , a kind of *h* pushed very heavily from the back of the mouth, but without any friction. The second kind of *h* (ه), which is like the English one, is symbolized by **h** with no dot.

kh (خ) is like the *ch* in Scottish *loch*, or in German *Buch.*

gh (غ) is pronounced in the same way as the above, but with voicing, i.e., vibration of the vocal chords.

' (ع) is a sound totally alien to English. It is a forcing of the air through a constriction in the throat, like a kind of backward gulp. If you cannot manage it, substitute *a* as in *cat.*

· (ء) is a glottal stop, a brief catching of the breath in the throat, as the Cockney *t* in *matter.*

q (ق) is properly pronounced as a kind of *k* far back in the mouth, but in the Fayoum, as in Cairo, it is nearly always replaced by a glottal stop. Thus *Qarûn* is usually pronounced *·arûn.*

sh (ش) is pronounced as in English *sheep.*

g (ج) is pronounced as in English *go.*

Other consonants are pronounced as in English.
Note that doubling of a consonant letter indicates that a consonant is long, and must be held for twice the normal time, as the *k* sound in English *bookcase*.

Vowels

The vowels are even more difficult to characterize in English than the consonants, and inconsistencies will inevitably arise, which the reader will kindly forgive.
The short vowels are marked as follows:
a either as in English *cat* or, when in the vicinity of an emphatic consonant, as something nearer to the *o* in English *cot*
e as in English *get*
i as in English *hit*
u as in English *pull*
With the length mark ˆ, these become:
â either as *ai* in English *fair* or as *a* in English *card*
î as in English *bead*
ê something like the *ai* in English *laid*, but much tighter
û as in English *cool*
There is also a long ô, like the *oa* in *road*, but tighter.

The spelling of 'Fayoum' used in this book is one widely used by English speakers and by the Egyptian government. The systematic transcription would be Fayyûm.

Certain key names and words are also given in Arabic script. Those familiar with Arabic will perhaps prefer to read these, ignoring the transcription. Those with no knowledge of Arabic might use them to point to when in difficulty.

The Fayoum Now

باردة الأسحار، بارزة الأشجار، كثيرة الثمار، قليلة الأمطار

"Cool are the dawns; tall are the trees; many are the fruits; little are the rains."

Not the earliest description of the Fayoum by a foreigner, but certainly one of the most poetic. The words were written quite recently—around 750 years ago, in fact—by a former governor of the Fayoum, Abu 'Uthmân al-Nabulsi. Although during his brief stay this Syrian amir conceived no liking for the inhabitants of the region, he was impressed by the richness and beauty of the land, parts of which reminded him of the gardens of Damascus.

Other visitors, long before and long after Nabulsi, have also written in praise of the Fayoum as "a true earthly paradise," "the garden of Egypt," "paradise of the desert." The stress has always been on the fertility and beauty of the land—by no means the only attraction of the Fayoum to the modern visitor, but surely attraction enough, especially after the concrete desert of Cairo.

Whether the reason for the visit be business, archaeology, pleasure, or a little of each, Nabulsi's cool dawns, tall trees, many fruits, and dry climate are bound to charm. So too will the kaleidoscope of lush orchards, slender palms, fields of golden barley, yellow-flowered cotton, or ripe-red tomatoes; of twisting, busy streams; of skylarks singing high in the sharp, clean air; of the lazy, satisfied plod of the buffalo going home at sunset; of the flourishing mustaches of the farmers; of the song and splash of the waterwheels; of a hundred and one other reflections of the richness and beauty that pervade the entire province.

The Fayoum has other treasures—a great salt lake, prehistoric whales, ancient temples, pyramids, and ruined towns, old mosques and monasteries, bazaars and markets, legends and traditions, colorful festivals, a variety of intriguing placenames—Cake, Paste, The Steamer, The Stone, The Fight—and a treasure that Governor Nabulsi unfortunately failed to appreciate: friendly, warmhearted people.

Topography

On the map, the Fayoum appears as the bud of the great lotus plant of Egypt, growing out of one side of the Nile stem, just below the Delta blossom. Not part of either the Nile Valley or the Delta, it cannot be ascribed to Upper, Lower, or even Middle Egypt. Nor does it conform to the usual idea of an oasis, since it is entirely dependent on water from the Nile. Thus it has a kind of dual identity: part desert oasis, part Nile Valley, yet not quite either. It rather resembles an unborn fetus, having almost the form of an individual being, but still vitally linked by the umbilical cord of the Baḥr Yûsuf to the Mother Nile.

The Fayoum is a large, natural depression in the Western Desert of Egypt, similar in formation to others such as the larger Qaṭṭâra Depression, but differing from these others in having a direct water supply from the Nile and a rich soil of Nilotic silt. It lies between 29° 5′ and 29° 35′ north (that is, about 6° north of the Tropic of Cancer) and between 30° 22′ and 31° 5′ east, and has a total area of about 4,000 square kilometers. The northern part of the depression is entirely below sea level and contains a large, salty lake, Birkat Qarûn (the Birka), which lies at around 45 meters below sea level, with slight seasonal fluctuations. The greatest depth of the Birka is 8 meters. It has a surface area of 214 square kilometers, and contains around 800 cubic kilometers of water. Golden Horn Island, with an area of about 2 square kilometers, lies approximately in the middle of the Birka. Cultivation extends to the southern shore of the Birka, but the northern shore is barren.

Nile water enters the depression via the Baḥr Yûsuf, a canalized river, which used to draw directly from the Nile, but now draws from the nineteenth-century Ibrahîmiya Canal at Dayrût in Asyûṭ governorate and runs roughly parallel to the Nile on its west side for nearly 300 kilometers before reaching the Fayoum. The Baḥr Yûsuf leaves the Nile Valley at Beni Swêf and flows through the narrow Lahûn Gap, the Fayoum's umbilical cord, to enter the depression at its highest point, about 23 meters above sea level. From here, the land slopes away to the north and southwest in a delta formation, and channels branch off from the Baḥr Yûsuf at various points to radiate all over the depression, though none reaches the Birka.

While the farmland of Egypt's Nile Valley and Delta is almost all monotonously flat, the land of the Fayoum, though also flat in parts, often rises and falls quite idiosyncratically within its general declivity toward the Birka, and is cut through by several steep-sided, twisting valleys that carry rushing streams more or less northward. The vertical dimension to the Fayoumi landscape has led to extensive terrace cultivation, a sight particularly appealing as it is so rare elsewhere in Egypt.

The Fayoum has an entirely closed drainage system, there being no outlet to the sea. Two main drains, which have cut deep, picturesque valleys, the Maṣraf al-Wâdi in the west and the Maṣraf al-Baṭs in the east, take most of the excess water down to the Birka, where it is lost through evaporation and possibly some seepage.

The depression is bounded on the northwest by a high limestone scarp, elsewhere by elevated desert or low hills, broken only by the thin green strip (one and a half kilometers at its narrowest) of the Lahûn Gap.

To the southwest of the Fayoum is a smaller depression, Wâdi al-Rayyân, reaching 43 meters below sea level. This has no natural water supply and no soil, but water has recently been channeled in to form two large lakes, and land is being reclaimed (see page 64).

Climate

The climate of the Fayoum is probably one of the most agreeable in Egypt. Summers are not as hot as those in Upper Egypt and winters are not as wet as those in Cairo and Lower Egypt. In high summer (June to August) the afternoon temperature is usually around 36°C, with a minimum temperature at night of around 20°. Heat waves lasting a few days may push these figures up to over 40° and 30° respectively, which is very uncomfortable, but these are mercifully quite rare. Most of the time a good breeze helps to keep things cool. Winter (December to February) usually sees maximum temperatures of between 15° and 20°, and minimums of between 5° and 10°. Rain can fall any time between October and May, though it is most likely in December, January, and February, and is nearly always light and short-lived.

The month of Amshîr (early February to early March) often brings very cold, northerly gales that raise dust and sand and chill the bones. The Khamsîn is a similar dust- and sand-laden wind that can blow in from the southwest any time between March and May, but this one is hot, and can be extremely unpleasant. There is nothing to do but stay locked up indoors and sit it out. Be careful when going out in or after a Khamsîn, as the temperature can drop dramatically when it is over.

Take note in summer that although the sun often does not burn in towns like Cairo and Fayoum because of the dust in the atmosphere, air in the country or in the desert is much cleaner, and fair skin scorches very rapidly. Short sleeves or low necks are not recommended on country or desert trips; hats and sunscreen are.

Human Geography

The whole Fayoum depression and the narrow strip of the Lahûn Gap are under the jurisdiction of one central governing body, the Fayoum Governorate, whose administrative borders stretch well into the desert beyond the depression and the limits of cultivation. The total area of the governorate is 4,578 square kilometers, or 1,089,564 feddân.

The inhabited area is broken down into six administrative 'centers' *(markaz)*, based around the six 'cities' of the Fayoum: Sinnûris and Ibshawây in the north, Yûsuf al-Ṣiddîq in the northwest, Ṭâmiya in the northeast, Iṭsa in the south, and Fayoum in the center. At the next administrative level come the 163 'villages' *(qarya)*, each of which has an appointed *'umda*, a kind of mayor-cum-sheriff who is responsible for representing the government in his community, settling disputes, and keeping a general peace. The authority of an *'umda* covers not only the main village, but also any of the 1,879 'hamlets' *('izba)* that lie within the village boundaries. A hamlet is basically any nuclear settlement too small to have its own *'umda.*

The latest census figures available, from 2006, give the total population of the governorate as 2,512,792 (about 3 percent of the total population of Egypt), with an annual growth rate of 2.5 percent (projected to 2008, this gives a figure of around 2.64 million). Of this total, 28.5 percent of the population lives in the six cities, the remainder in the villages and hamlets. Rural population tends to be most dense in the central areas of the depression, sparser in the fringe areas near the desert.

The people of the Fayoum usually classify themselves in two main ethnic groups—a majority of 'Egyptians' in the towns and central areas, and a minority of settled 'Bedouin' or 'Arabs' in the peripheral areas. The Bedouin are generally very conscious of their separate identity, and proud of it, referring to the ethnic Egyptians disparagingly as 'pharaonic.' There are also groups of semi-nomadic Bedouin who live a very simple existence in tents, herding sheep and goats, and keep themselves totally separate from the rest of the population. Both the Egyptians and the settled Bedouin refer to these groups as 'gypsies' *(ghagar).*

The proximity of the Fayoum to Cairo makes it possible for a large number of Fayoumis to work in the capital, returning to the Fayoum at weekends for home comforts and home cooking. These commuters include all kinds of workers, from laborers to doctors. Another large class of weekly commuters are the students attending university colleges and institutes in Cairo, where the variety of studies is much greater. Recently, however, educational opportunities at home have increased and Fayoum now has its own university, with thirteen faculties, including Education, Archaeology, Tourism and Hotels, and Medicine, attended by 25,000 students.

Water, Irrigation, and Drainage

The water supply to the Fayoum is strictly regulated at al-Lahûn, at the point where the Baḥr Yûsuf leaves the Nile Valley to enter the Fayoum via the Lahûn Gap by a system of locks and sluices. Excess water is diverted northeastward along the Gîza Canal, while the amount required by the Fayoum is allowed through in the Baḥr Yûsuf and into its first main distributary, the Baḥr Ḥasan Wâṣif, which runs parallel to it along the Lahûn Gap. The amount of water entering the Fayoum varies according to the season, with a maximum during the rice season (spring to summer) and a minimum in winter. For twenty days in January every year the sluices at al-Lahûn are shut and the Fayoum's entire canal system dries up to 'let the land rest' and to allow for the cleaning and maintenance of waterways, bridge-building, and so on.

The main distribution point for the water is at the western end of Fayoum city, where the Baḥr Yûsuf splits down into eight channels, which then go off in different directions and develop into a radial network supplying the whole cultivated area. Government figures once quoted a total of 234 canals in the Fayoum, measuring altogether 1,296 kilometers, and a further 222 drainage channels with a combined length of 924 kilometers. The total length of waterways would take you from Fayoum to Rome.

This proliferation of water courses is necessitated by the system of irrigation now employed in the Fayoum, as in most parts of Egypt, called perennial irrigation. Previously, large parts of the Fayoum were under the simpler system of basin irrigation, whereby parcels of land were enclosed by embankments or walls (like the one at Shidmôh—see page 85) and water was fed in by one main canal, to a depth of a meter or so, left to stand for some time, then run off. Crops were planted, nurtured, and harvested without further watering. This method required only a very simple canal system, which was obviously easy and cheap to maintain, but allowed for only one crop per year. Late in the nineteenth century, basin irrigation was superseded in all parts by perennial irrigation, which involves a much more complex (and expensive) system of canals, branch canals, small channels, and runlets, capable of taking a regulated amount of water to any individual field. This means a farmer can plant and irrigate at any time of the year and bring in two or perhaps three crops.

With the water supply entering the Fayoum depression at its highest point, optimum use can be made of the gradient of the land, so that with careful routing of water courses, gravity can do most of the work in distributing the water, and it rarely needs to be lifted. When the water does need to be raised, farmers use either a motorized pump or a *saqya* (waterwheel). The *saqya* is of two types—one drawing from a well, using cogs and animal power (usually a blindfolded cow or donkey); the other, the type for which the Fayoum is renowned, drawing directly from a canal and driven by the force of the canal itself (see page 42). The Nile Valley *shadûf* is not used at all in the Fayoum, while the *ṭunbûr* (Archimedes' screw), also extensively used in the Valley, is very rare.

The upkeep of all waterways, sluices, and waterwheels is the responsibility of the government irrigation department, which also works out and supervises a precise rota for the allocation of water to individual farmers. This is to ensure that everybody gets their fair share and nobody loses out. Each farmer is allotted a fixed period per week in which to take water from a certain canal. The time allowed per feddân of land per week may vary from half an hour to three or four hours, depending on the distance of the land from the water supply. The farmer is given a set time on a certain day in which to take his water once a week. If he does not finish irrigating in that time, he forfeits his right and the channel is closed. If he prefers, he can water once a fortnight or once a month, being allowed the sum of his weekly rations. This can be useful with certain crops such as cotton, which requires water only once every two weeks.

Because of the strict rota, some farmers have to take their water at night. One morning, when I went to visit a friend in a small hamlet near al-Gharaq, I was surprised to find him still asleep at eleven o'clock. He explained that he had been planting tomatoes until three in the morning on his cousin's land, because this man's water rights came at night, and tomatoes must be planted when the soil is wet. Luckily, they had had a full moon to see by.

In other parts of Egypt, drainage water can be returned to the Nile, which can cope with the excess by emptying it into the Mediterranean. As the Fayoum has no outlet either back to the Nile or out to sea, drainage in the depression presents special problems. Until recently, all drainage water was taken by one of the two main drainage channels, Maṣraf al-Wâdi or Maṣraf al-Baṭs, or one of the other minor ones, down to Birkat Qarûn in the north, to be lost by evaporation. The Birka, however, can take only a certain volume of drainage water to balance its rate of evaporation, which is calculated at 370 million cubic meters per year. Any drainage water over that amount causes the lake level to rise and flood surrounding land, often doing irreparable damage because of the water's high salt content. This means that the amount of water that can be used in the Fayoum is strictly limited, not by a shortage of supply, but by a maximum drainage capacity, with the consequence until recently that water-intensive crops such as rice and reeds could be grown only in very small quantities, and that no new land could be reclaimed without causing swamping of existing farmland near the lake.

An ambitious project designed to overcome this problem was begun in 1974. A watercourse, consisting of a 9-kilometer open channel and an 8-kilometer tunnel, was cut through the desert from the western side of the Fayoum depression to the large, dry depression of Wâdi al-Rayyân, west of the Fayoum. Drainage water now flows to Wâdi al-Rayyân, where two lakes have formed that have a combined surface area of some 30,000 feddân. The scheme was designed to bring a number of important benefits to the governorate. Without causing swamping or flooding around Birkat Qarûn, more land in the Fayoum basin can now be reclaimed and existing farmland turned over to increased production of rice and of reeds for the local mat-making industry, and large areas of desert in Wâdi al-Rayyân itself are being reclaimed for agriculture, while the lakes are being developed for fishing and tourism. It is hoped that the Rayyân project will eventually support 900,000 people through farming, fishing, industry, or tourism.

Agriculture

The 1878 edition of Baedeker calls the Fayoum the "land of roses" and poetically notes that "the beautiful rich-colored red roses of the gardens of the Fayoum, which were once so lavishly strewn at the banquets of Cleopatra, still thrive here." Other early writers mention the famous roses of the Fayoum, but unfortunately farming habits have changed, and Cleopatra's roses have finally disappeared, although pale pink 'baladi' roses do flower along the road from Fidimîn to Sanhûr. As for other crops of former times, Strabo (first century BCE) talks of olives, grapes, "as well as grain, pulse and other seed-plants in very great varieties." Nabulsi (thirteenth century CE) writes about "magnificent orchards and gardens" producing figs, pears, apples, apricots, dates, grapes, carob, mulberry, jasmine, and water-lilies, and lists a whole variety of other crops including wheat, barley, beans, flax, lentils, onions, lupins, kidney beans, sesame, indigo, turnips, and cabbages. The main summer crop was sugar cane, while cotton was grown only in small quantities—today the reverse is true. In the fifteenth century, the province was an important center for wool and flax. The fields of the nineteenth-century Fayoum yielded, according to Baedeker, rice, sugar, cotton, flax, and hemp, "besides the usual cereals."

Today, the 423,737 feddân (1,780 square kilometers) of cultivated land in the Fayoum support a wide variety of crops, changing according to the season, the area and type of soil, the preferences of the individual farmer, and the quotas of the government. The main cash crop of the region is cotton, whose cultivation is carefully controlled by the government. It is planted in April and harvested in September, and is grown mostly in the central areas of the Fayoum. In the peripheral areas, where the soil is sandier, the favorite crop tends to be tomatoes, grown from September to April. Many medicinal and aromatic plants are also grown in the peripheral areas, and are considered quite lucrative crops. These include camomile, mint, marigold, sunflowers, fenugreek, and sesame, which is reckoned to be one of the most profitable crops of all.

A great deal of land is given over in winter to the cultivation of *barsîm*, a kind of clover. *Barsîm* is a domestic crop, produced usually to feed the farmer's own animals, but a farmer with a surplus can sell it locally for a good price. It is a prolific crop, allowing four or five cuttings per season. Other seasonal crops include wheat, beans, maize, rice, melons, watermelons, cucumbers, pepper, onions, garlic, potatoes, zucchini, eggplants, cauliflower, and cabbage. Sugar cane, so common in Upper Egypt, is rarely seen in the Fayoum.

About 500 feddân are taken up with palms, although in the Fayoum they tend not to be concentrated in palm groves, as for instance in the New Valley oases, but usually grow dotted around a farmer's land or along canals. Every part of the palm, which must be one of the most versatile plants in the world, is utilized. The fruit, produced by the female tree, is eaten; the fingers of the fronds are used for making baskets, the spines for making crates and covering roofs; the whole fronds are sold to mourners to place on tombs and are used in the construction of mud enclosure walls and for roofing; the fiber is turned into rope and brushes; the trunk can be split and used for roof-beams and bridges; and the white 'heart' of the palm is considered a special delicacy to be offered to honored guests.

Over 17,000 feddân (around 70 square kilometers), mostly in the central areas, are devoted to fruit-growing, and it is from these orchards that the Fayoum earns its 'Garden of Egypt' title. The orchards usually contain several varieties, and the mixture of trees of different shapes, sizes, and greens behind the simple mud and palm-frond walls often makes a very attractive scene. The area around Fidimîn, al-Siliyîn, and Sanhûr is particularly noted for its rich orchards producing oranges, lemons, mandarins, guavas, mangos, pears, apples, plums, figs, and apricots. There are also a few banana plantations and vineyards, and olives are extensively cultivated along the south shore of the western end of Birkat Qarûn. The large cactus plants scattered around the orchards produce the prickly pear ('thorny fig' in Arabic) in summer. All these fruits are sold fresh on the streets of Fayoum in their respective seasons, and large quantities are transported to Cairo and other parts of Egypt.

A number of animals are regularly kept by the Fayoumi farmer. Donkeys are kept by most as all-around beasts of burden and means of transport. Cattle are often used as work-animals (pulling ploughs, turning waterwheels), while the main dairy animal is the buffalo, which produces very creamy milk. The milk can be sold or used at home, or turned into a gamut of dairy products: cream, butter, ghee, white cheese, old cheese (cheese stored in whey in a sealed container for several months), sour milk, curds, whey, or the delicious *mish* (hot pepper whey, served with old cheese). The favorite meat animal is the sheep (the Middle Eastern fat-tailed variety), though goats are occasionally kept, and steer buffaloes are slaughtered young. Chickens provide eggs and meat, and ducks, geese, and pigeons are also kept for the table. Camels are quite rare in the Fayoum, their price putting them beyond the means of most small farmers.

Buffaloes are also very expensive, but a neat system operates to the mutual benefit of poor farmers and rich investors. The investor (who may be a farmer himself with spare cash, or a landowner, or a town-dweller with country connections) buys a buffalo and gives it to a farmer to keep. The farmer feeds the animal at his expense, and uses or sells all the milk except a small proportion taken by the owner. If the animal calves, the profit from the calf is split equally between the farmer and the investor, and when the buffalo itself comes to be sold, any profit over the original cost of the animal is also divided equally. This practice, also applicable to cattle and camels, is very common in the Fayoum.

Good land in the Fayoum can command a stiff price, but land need not always be sold. Many farmers without land rent it from people who either do not want to farm it themselves or who cannot afford the capital to buy seeds and fertilizer, but simply live on the rent from the land. A farmer with no land is not necessarily poor, while a landowner with several feddân is not necessarily rich.

Farmers sow and reap and reckon the year according to a calendar that is directly descended from that used by the ancient Egyptians. They often have a passing knowledge of the Western calendar and of the Islamic one (which, being lunar, has no connection with the farming seasons), but the one they work and live by is much older than both. The year consists of twelve months of thirty days each and a short month of five or six days at the end of the year. It begins with the month of Tût on September 11, the time when, before the building of the High Dam, the Nile flood used to reach its peak. The first four months constitute the Nile flood season; the second four, starting with Ṭûba, winter; and the third four, starting with Bashons, summer. Every rural activity has its rightful place in the calendar, as does the weather. Ṭûba is the coldest month, while its successor Amshîr is known for its strong winds. Some time around the end of Kiyâk and the beginning of Ṭûba, the farmers, halfway through the tomato harvest, await with dread the coming of Abu Zuqm (rough translation: 'Old Gobbler'), a sharp snap of three or four days of bitter cold, with frost at night, which can kill tomato plants and other crops and damage the ripening tomatoes.

One of the major hazards of Egyptian rural life has all but disappeared from the Fayoum. Fayoumi farmers have a German chemical company, Bayer, and their chemical, Bilocide, to thank for making the Fayoum the first practically Bilharzia-free zone in the country.

Other Rural Occupations

Fayoumi chickens are reputed to be the best in Egypt and have become proverbial. Chicken-farming in the Fayoum is treated more as an industry than as a branch of the traditional agricultural pattern. Specialized poultry stations are private, cooperative, or government enterprises, and between them produce several million chickens a year. The chickens are bred for either eggs or meat, and the Fayoum's proximity to Cairo provides a large and easily accessible market.

Numerous apiaries around the Fayoum, often situated in orchards or olive groves, represent another profitable rural business. Fayoum honey is very good and sells all over the country. There is also a fluctuating perfume industry, based on geraniums, the essence of which is extracted locally by water and steam. Other small-scale manufacturing concerns produce pottery, baskets, rush mats, rugs, and ropes.

Fishing is an old industry in the Fayoum. Birkat Qarûn was known in the thirteenth century as Birkat al-Ṣêd, the Fishing Lake, and was renowned for its stocks of fish. One winter's night in 1245, a cold gale blew, chilling the lake and causing the deaths of thousands and thousands of fish. A canal overseer reported that he walked the next day from morning until night along the lake shore and all the way along found fish in layers of different species, stacked up like the bricks of a house, while birds and animals feasted on the miraculous windfall. Despite this obvious abundance, only thirty fishing boats operated on the Birka at that time. At the beginning of the nineteenth century, a French visitor (see page 29) was told that the local population did not fish on the Birka at all, but that fishermen from the Nile came every year to ply their nets from the end of March until the Nile flood.

Today, the lake water has become too salty for most of the original species of Nile fish, though the *bulṭi* remains and is said to be better than *bulṭi* from the Nile itself. In order to compensate for the dwindling stocks of freshwater fish, certain species of marine fish, like mullet, eel, sole, and shrimps, have been introduced with varying degrees of success, and a research station at Shakshûk studies which other species would do well in the Birka. Outside the closed season (mid-April to mid-June), several hundred boats fish the salty waters. A cooperative provides nets, boats, and loans to promote the industry. Fishing is also promoted on the new Wâdi al-Rayyân lakes, where Nile carp and Nile perch have been introduced.

Industry

The Fayoum is, of course, predominantly an agricultural area, supporting mostly agriculture-related activities, so industry plays a relatively small part in the life of the province. There is a major cotton-mill at al-'Azab, which provides employment for a large number of people, and there are canning plants for apricots and tomatoes at Biahmu and Ṭâmiya. A new industrial area is now well established at Kôm Ôshîm, including several large factories producing ceramic tiles.

An animal feed mill operates at Sinnûris, and a large salt extraction plant on the Birka west of Shakshûk produces sodium chloride, sodium sulphate, sodium sulphide, magnesium oxide, and potassium for both local use and export. The mineral water bottling plant that was opened at al-Siliyîn in 1984 at the expense of a beautiful area of palm groves is permanently closed due to production difficulties. A sugar factory has been opened south of Tuṭûn for processing sugar beet–Fayoumi farmers previously had to transport their crop all the way to a processing plant at Kafr al-Shêkh in the Nile Delta.

Certain raw materials are found in commercial quantities in the deserts around the Fayoum: clay, used in the brick and cement industries; limestone, used in the cement industry; sand and gravel for building; basalt at Gebel Qaṭrâni, north of the Birka, which was quarried in dynastic times; white sand, used in the glass industry; and gypsum. There are also small deposits of oil.

Local Crafts

Most of the ornamental baskets *(sabat)* that are persistently hawked in Fayoum town center, at 'În al-Siliyîn, and at Birkat Qarûn are made in al-A'lâm, the first village out of Fayoum on the Cairo road. In many houses of the village, groups of women sit on the floor, deftly fashioning the characteristic baskets. Bundles of rice straw are sewn in a continuous spiral with palm leaf fingers, pushed through with substantial steel needles. The final results, in all different shapes and sizes, often with fancy patterns in red or green, are both attractive and tough, and last for years. In al-'Agamiyîn, a village to the northwest of Fayoum on the road to Ibshawây, another type of basket is made, called *ma·ṭaf.* This is a soft, open basket made of woven palm leaf fingers, used by Egyptian laborers and farmers for moving earth, mud, rocks, and so on. The *ma·ṭaf* has a very old pedigree: in a showcase on the right as you enter the Kôm Ôshîm Museum is a 2,000-year-old terracotta model of one, found among the nearby ruins of the Ptolemaic town of Karanis. Also at al-'Agamiyîn, multipurpose crates are made from the spines of palm leaves, while rope and rope nets are made from palm fiber.

Portrait of a woman from Hawwâra, second century CE, now in the Egyptian Museum, Cairo *(photograph by Araldo De Luca/WhiteStar Archives)*

In the fields near Biahmu

One of the Fayoum's distinctive terraced valleys

Marigold fields near Ibshawây

Farming on the shores of Birkat Qarûn

Waterwheels on the Baḥr Sinnûris

The southern lake
of Wâdi al-Rayyân,
from Gebel al-Nuhûd

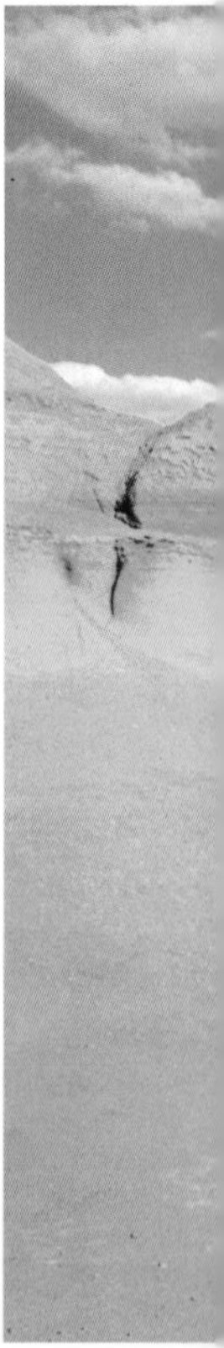

Greater flamingoes
at the western end
of Birkat Qarûn

The 40-million-year-old
skeleton of a whale
at Wâdi al-Ḥitân

Feet of a goddess
at Madînat Mâḍi

The cave church of Dêr Wâdi al-Rayyân

The southern temple at Karanis, Kôm Ôshîm

One of the eleventh-century wall paintings at Dêr al-Malâk

Plain, utilitarian pottery goods are made in several places, but particularly renowned is the village of al-Nazla, south of Ibshawây, picturesquely situated on the cliff of one of the Fayoum's two main drainage streams, Maṣraf al-Wâdi, the 'Valley Drain,' which is much more beautiful than its prosaic name implies. Along the cliff, between the village and the valley floor, a fascinating jumble of potters' huts and kilns takes up every available level space. Around about, the fresh mud-and-straw pots, large and round, are left to dry in the sun before being baked. On Tuesdays in Fayoum a whole range of pots, red or pink and unglazed, is to be found in a special market just off Schools Street *(shâri' al-madâris)* in the northwest of the city. The village of Tûnis, near the western end of the Birka, is home to three ceramic artists, two of whom have set up a pottery school in the village (see page 57).

Fidimîn, a village just north of al-Siliyîn, is well known as the center of the main fruit-growing area of the province, but it has another interest, which is its local crafts center, on the left when traveling from Fayoum, next to a school and just opposite the Fidimîn rural hospital. It serves as a training center for local children to become skilled in weaving, tapestry, embroidery, or beadwork, and also markets their produce, both while they are working in the center and after they have left to work at home. The carpets woven by the boys on looms imported from Finland are made of pure wool on cotton warp, and come in many different abstract designs, either in brightly dyed colors or in natural browns, blacks, grays, and creams. The girls make intricate bead necklaces and produce fine tapestry and embroidery work. The center is open to visitors Monday to Thursday, 8–2.

Wildlife

The wildlife of the Fayoum, particularly in the quieter areas of the countryside, is quite varied. Of the larger mammals, foxes are often seen, even in the towns, and jackals are fairly common in the desert. Although jackals are generally shy of humans, they are probably a good reason for not being alone in the desert at night. In quiet fields and orchards you may sometimes see an Egyptian mongoose running low or silently listening with its head high. Unfortunately, you are more likely to see one, minus its insides, displayed as a trophy on the front of a car.

The rarest of the large mammals is probably the *·uṭṭat al-ghêṭ*, or swamp cat, a dull gray-brown cat about twice the size of its domestic cousin. I had heard of the animal, but it was more than three years before I saw even a dead one, and several months more before I finally saw a live one in a field just outside Fayoum town, near the Seven Waterwheels. Looking like a small lynx, it was creeping stealthily along the edge of the field. When it suddenly became aware of me, it stopped and stared for a moment, not frightened, then slid away into the undergrowth of the ditch.

The most common bird, as almost anywhere else in Egypt, is the cattle egret, *abu qurdân*, no less beautiful for its ubiquity. Thousands of *abu qurdân* roost in the palms and trees around the village of al-Ka'âbi al-Gadîda (on the old Cairo road between Sinnûris and Fayoum), giving the appearance of prolific white blossom among the branches. A relative of the egret, the gray heron, is sometimes seen along canals; it is known in Arabic as 'the sad king.' The wide-eyed, long-legged stone-curlew lives in the deserts, while other waders and ducks are found on the Birka. Winter visitors to the Birka include spoonbills and spectacular flocks of greater flamingo, which feed in the shallows at the western end; the local fishermen call them—quite appropriately—*warrâd*, from the root relating to 'rose'; in ancient Egyptian, the word for flamingo was also the word for 'red.' In the countryside there are skylarks, wagtails, Egyptian swallows (differing from the European variety in having entirely red underparts), bee-eaters, shrikes, and doves. Spur-winged plovers are almost as common as egrets. The hooded crow abounds, as do the kestrel and the black-shouldered kite. Little owls often roost in palms.

A very shy bird, occasionally sighted in tomato fields and palms, is the Senegal coucal *(mukk)*, a member of the cuckoo family. It is quite unmistakable—about the size of a crow, with a black head, light underparts, rufous wings, and a long tail. It has a heavy bill and beady red eyes, and hops about in a most ungainly but endearing way.

But the most engaging bird of the region is undoubtedly the giant, four-legged desert peacock. Plodding slowly along country lanes, head low, long thick green tail softly swaying, stirring the dust, a camel carrying a load of freshly cut palm-fronds really is more like some exotic, graceful bird than a beast of burden hard at work. The pity is that you will never see this magnificent creature in display posture.

History of the Fayoum

In ancient mythology, the great lake of the Fayoum was identified with Nun, the primeval ocean, the origin of all life, while the high land around the capital, Shedet, was the primeval hill where life first came into existence.

A legend recorded by Diodorus tells of King Menes (the semi-mythical uniter of Upper and Lower Egypt) on a hunting expedition in the Fayoum. His own dogs attacked him near the lake, but his life was saved by a crocodile, which carried him across the water to safety. In gratitude he declared the lake a sanctuary for crocodiles, and founded the city of Shedet (later Crocodilopolis, now Kimân Fâris), which became the cult center of the crocodile god Sobek. Sobek remained chief deity of the Fayoum throughout dynastic and Greek times and into the Roman era, and all temples were dedicated, or at least co-dedicated, to one or another of his aspects. A sacred crocodile kept at the main temple at Crocodilopolis was seen and described by both Herodotus and Strabo.

In early dynastic times, the Fayoum remained undeveloped, much of it probably marsh and swamp, but it was popular as a hunting-ground in royal circles, never more so than in the halcyon Twelfth Dynasty, when a number of kings of that family, resident at al-Lisht̩ nearby in the Nile Valley, developed a special attachment to the province. It was probably the founder of the Twelfth Dynasty, Amenemhat I, who, in the first half of the twentieth century BCE, flooded the Fayoum to create the famous Lake Moeris, described 1,500 years later by Herodotus. The second king of the line, Senwosret I, erected the obelisk of Abgîg, and Lahûn pyramid is the tomb of Senwosret II. Amenemhat III had a long

In the Fayoum		In Egypt
		c.3200 BCE Unification of Upper and Lower Egypt
The Fayoum mostly lake and marsh; the capital Shedet (Kimân Fâris) a cult center for crocodile god Sobek	3000 BCE	
	Old Kingdom	c.2700–2600 BCE Great Pyramids of Gîza
	First Intermediate Period	
Enlargement of Lake Moeris; obelisk of Abgîg; pyramids of al-Lahûn, Hawwâra; Madînat Mâḍi; al-Ṣanam; Qaṣr al-Ṣâgha	2000 BCE	c.2000 BCE 12th Dynasty founded by Amenemhat I
	Middle Kingdom	c.1790 End of 12th Dynasty
	Second Intermediate Period	
	New Kingdom	c.1350 Tutankhamun dies
Extensions to Shedet by Ramesses II		
	1000	
Large-scale reclamation, many foreign settlers; height of the Fayoum's prosperity; Qaṣr Qarûn, Karanis, Dimêh al-Sibâ'	Ptolemaic Period	c.440 Herodotus visits Egypt
		30 Egypt becomes Roman province
		c.30 Strabo visits Egypt
	BCE	
	CE	
Loss of land and abandonment of many towns	Roman Period	
	Byzantine Period	395 Roman Empire splits in two
		451 Egyptian church splits from Byzantine
Dêr al-Malâk founded		640–41 Arab conquest of Egypt
		969 Fatimid conquest of Egypt
	1000	
		1169–93 Ṣalâḥ al-Dîn (Saladin)
Nabulsi		
Qâytbây mosque and bridge		
		1517 Start of Ottoman rule
Lucas, Pococke		
Martin		1798–1801 Napoleonic French in Egypt
Settling of Bedouin		1805–48 Muḥammad 'Ali
		1952 Free Officers' Revolution
Flooding of Wâdi al-Rayyân	2000	

and peaceful reign around the end of the nineteenth century BCE, and left a number of monuments including the colossi of Biahmu (al-Ṣanam), temples at Madînat Mâḍi and Kimân Fâris, and at Hawwâra the great Labyrinth and his own pyramid, the only pyramid built away from the Nile Valley. His successor, Amenemhat IV, also left his mark at the temple of Madînat Mâḍi.

After this golden age, interest in the Fayoum dropped off until the advent of the Ptolemies and their Greek rule in pharaoh's clothing, which began with the death of Alexander the Great in 323 BCE. Ptolemy I started to drain Lake Moeris, and reclaimed about 1,200 square kilometers of excellent land. The work was continued by his son, Ptolemy II Philadelphus, who gave parcels of the new and very fertile land to his Greek and Macedonian veterans, who settled in considerable numbers in the province. Ptolemy II, who reigned from 285 to 246 BCE, shocked the Greek world by following Egyptian practice and marrying his sister Arsinoë II. Arsinoë became a very popular queen and was genuinely mourned by her people when she died in 270. Ptolemy himself was known as a wise and cultured ruler–it was he who founded the celebrated Library of Alexandria. The reclamation and settlement drives gave the Fayoum a fresh breath of life, and the province blossomed into probably the richest and most productive area of the country. The fertile land and the hard work and new techniques of the settlers combined to give birth to the 'Garden of Egypt.' One of the lasting innovations of the settlers was the water-propelled *saqya*, now the hallmark of the Fayoum.

The settlers were mostly Greeks and Macedonians, but also included groups of Jews, Persians, Arabs, Syrians, Thracians, and Samaritans. Unlike the Greeks of Alexandria, the Greeks of the Fayoum soon began to intermarry with the native Egyptians. The other nationalities did the same, as well as intermarrying with the Greeks and with each other, so while the Alexandrian Greeks remained a homogeneous community for a long time, the Fayoum became a great melting-pot in which racial purity could not survive.

Ptolemy named one of the new settlements on the eastern fringe of the Fayoum Philadelphia, 'brotherly love,' in reference to his sister–wife

Arsinoë. He also renamed the whole province in her honor, calling it the Arsinoite nome, with its capital (formerly Crocodilopolis) Arsinoë. Her posthumous deification was popularly accepted, and a great Arsinoëia festival was held annually in the Fayoum in the month of Misra (August).

Egypt became a Roman province after falling to Augustus in 30 BCE, and the prosperity of the Fayoum continued for some time, but as the great empire became unstable and began to disintegrate, the Fayoum went into decline. Under corrupt local government and mismanagement and an atmosphere of general economic depression, the irrigation system, a Ptolemaic triumph, gradually fell into disrepair, and good land was lost, much of it forever, to the desert. Many flourishing towns and villages in areas where land was lost–Karanis, Bacchias, Philadelphia, Tebtunis, Dionysias–declined, fell, and were abandoned between the third and fifth centuries CE.

In 395 CE the Roman Empire was partitioned, and Egypt became subject to the eastern emperor, ruling from Byzantium. Christianity had become the official religion of the empire, but the Egyptian church split with the Byzantine in 451 over a doctrinal issue. As a result, Byzantine rule became even less popular than it had previously been, and most Egyptians welcomed the Arab conquest of the caliph 'Umar when it came in 640, in the belief that the new regime could not be more repressive than the old.

The Fayoum, however, held out against the Arab armies and was one of the last parts of the country to fall. The province was defended by a Byzantine garrison and a native Egyptian force led by John of Maros, stationed at al-Lahûn. When the Arabs threatened Bahnasa (Oxyrhynchus), south of Beni Swêf, John hurried south and managed to repulse them, though they soon returned with reinforcements and took the town. John and his men escaped and fled south to Asyûṭ, where they were subsequently routed and killed. Meanwhile, one Theodorus maintained the Fayoum and used it as a base for unsuccessful sorties against Bahnasa. By this time the rest of the country had been abandoned and the main Byzantine forces had retired to the citadel of Babylon (Old Cairo), leaving all of northern Egypt and much of the south in Arab hands.

Babylon fell, however, in April 641 when the Arabs received 4,000 Berber reinforcements. The fall of Babylon meant the end of resistance in the Fayoum also, for when Domentianus, prefect of the Fayoum, heard the news, he fled the province with his troops in the night, leaving only a token garrison at Fayoum town. Theodorus was away in Middle Egypt; the Arabs immediately fell on the Fayoum and took it easily. The small force in the fort could offer little resistance and were all killed, and the inhabitants of the Fayoum surrendered peacefully. At about the same time, the last pocket of resistance in Upper Egypt was wiped out. The first governor of the Fayoum under the Arabs was not an Arab at all, but a Copt, Philoxenos, who faithfully carried out his duty, which included levying the poll-tax, payable by all non-Muslims.

In spite of the downward course the Fayoum had followed in Roman times, it was still famed at the beginning of the Islamic era as a very rich province. Legend credits the Fayoum at that time with 360 villages (there are now 163), each of which could supply the whole of Egypt with food for one day. However, the province declined further and saw the next twelve centuries through in a very sorry state.

The Fayoum suffered badly under the invading Fatimid army. When these Shiite warriors from Tunisia first attempted to conquer Egypt in 914, they reached the Fayoum, invaded it, and devastated it before being repulsed and driven out of the country. In their second attempt five years later, they again invaded the Fayoum, this time also taking Alexandria and pushing into Upper Egypt as far as al-Ashmunên, south of al-Minya. Fayoum and Alexandria were sacked, but in the Fayoum the invaders succumbed to famine and plague and were consequently unable to gain the upper hand in a crucial battle at Gîza. After several engagements in the Fayoum and at Alexandria, the Egyptian army, with reinforcements from Mesopotamia, dislodged the Fatimids and sent them back home in the spring of 920. Forty-nine years later they returned and finally took the country.

At the end of the tenth century, the annual fiscal return of the Fayoum was 620,000 dinars. By the reign of Ṣalâḥ al-Dîn in the second half of the twelfth century, this figure had dropped to 145,162 dinars. Ṣalâḥ al-Dîn, incidentally, added yet more foreign blood to the melting-pot when he granted land in the Fayoum to some of his Kurdish and Turkish officers. This famous sultan, the Saladin of European history books, himself owned land in the province, around Ikhṣâṣ, southeast of Sinnûris.

In 1245, Abu 'Uthmân al-Nabulsi, a Syrian amir appointed governor of the Fayoum, wrote a book about the province, concentrating particularly on the irrigation system, which he found to be so neglected that it was hardly functioning at all. The Baḥr Yûsuf (then known as Baḥr Munha) was so badly silted up that water flowed into the Fayoum for only four months of the year, during the Nile flood season. Smaller canals were in a similar or worse state. Nabulsi discovered to his horror that nothing had been spent on canal maintenance for the previous hundred years, and set about improving the water supply by cutting new channels and clearing old ones. Shortly after Nabulsi's brief governorship, a new regulator was constructed at al-Lahûn, which was in use until the middle of the twentieth century and still stands intact (see page 93).

The nadir of the Fayoum's sad decline came under the Ottoman Turks, who controlled Egypt from 1517 to 1798. Ottoman rule was represented in the Fayoum by a qadi sent once a year from Istanbul. For the rest of the year, the qadi's deputy held a divan twice a week, attended by sixty Arab shêkhs. In 1634 the revenue from the Fayoum had dropped to a mere 56,000 dinars. Part of the cause of the province's sinking fortunes was the discovery of the Cape route to India, which seriously affected Egypt's economy as a whole; and part was its remoteness and difficulty of access, particularly during the flood season, which made it especially vulnerable to Bedouin and Berber raids. This problem of raids from the desert was not finally brought under control until the middle of the nineteenth century.

In July 1798, while Egypt was under the joint control of two Mamluk beys, Murâd and Ibrahîm, the French army of Napoleon Bonaparte invaded the country and defeated the two beys at the Battle of the Pyramids. Ibrahîm Bey fled to Syria, Murâd Bey retreated to Middle Egypt, where a French force of 5,000 men under General Louis Charles Antoine Desaix de Veygoux was sent to rout him. There followed an almost personal contest between the two determined men, Murâd Bey and General Desaix, all around Middle Egypt and the Fayoum. Desaix first of all tried a surprise attack on Murâd's camp at Bahnasa, but Murâd was forewarned by local farmers and slipped away. Desaix went south to Asyûṭ, gained the Baḥr Yûsuf, and sailed north for ten days. The journey was hard and eventually unrewarding, as Murâd once again escaped after a battle south of Beni Swêf. The next confrontation took place on October 7, 1798 at Sidmant, a little way southwest of al-Lahûn. The heavy battle was again indecisive. Desaix camped at al-Lahûn and then at Fayoum town, where he was held up for a month by an epidemic of conjunctivitis. Murâd attacked the debilitated garrison at Fayoum on November 8, but was repulsed. Desaix regrouped at Beni Swêf and followed Murâd into Upper Egypt, having promised Bonaparte that he would "spare no effort to destroy him."

Murâd retired to Nubia, leaving Desaix in control of Upper Egypt, but in 1799 he reappeared in the Fayoum. By this time, Bonaparte had left Egypt, and his deputy, Kléber, was negotiating for a French evacuation. Murâd's activities in and around the Fayoum were part of the pressure forcing Kléber to negotiate. In October, Desaix assembled two camel columns to march on Murâd in the Fayoum. One of them met Murâd again at Sidmant. Murâd took the offensive, was repelled and pursued, but yet again escaped.

Desaix never did succeed in destroying Murâd. Peace was made and Murâd was appointed governor of Upper Egypt for the Republic of France on May 30, 1800. Desaix left Egypt and died in the same year at the Battle of Marengo. Murâd died of the plague in Upper Egypt on April 22, 1801.

The small village of Garadu, west of Fayoum, is popularly said to take its name from the activities of the French army in the area. After the Battle of Fayoum in October 1798, the French forces regrouped at the village and took stock—*garadu* in Arabic—before moving off. The story, however interesting, is unfortunately not true: Garadu was recorded by Nabulsi in the thirteenth century.

In the vacuum created by the French departure of 1801, a power struggle developed between the Turks and the Mamluks. In the middle, playing off one against the other and eventually defeating both, was a brilliant, if ruthless, Albanian coffee-dealer from Macedonia, Muḥammad 'Ali. As in previous power struggles, the Fayoum suffered. In September 1806, Fayoum town was taken and sacked by the Mamluk Yasîn Bey, and a large part of the population was massacred for its support of Muḥammad 'Ali. Yasîn held the Fayoum for almost four years until Muḥammad retook it in July 1810. The following year, Muḥammad consolidated his power with the famous massacre of the Mamluks at the Cairo Citadel.

Muḥammad 'Ali revived the flagging economy with agricultural reforms, promoting the production of cotton as a cash crop in areas such as the Fayoum. He also went a long way to combatting the problem of raiding nomadic tribes. He first tried force—keeping hostages, recruiting tribesmen as irregulars into his army, requisitioning their horses—but met with little success. He then adopted a totally different and infinitely more successful strategy. In the 1830s he began appointing Bedouin shêkhs as district governors and granted them large tracts of land as private property to induce them to settle. The new approach was particularly successful in the Fayoum, where the problem had been serious. Here were settled large numbers of the troublesome Baraghîth tribe from Libya, who had arrived in Egypt in the previous century. Perhaps the cleverest part of Muḥammad 'Ali's settlement policy was that essential tribal unity was shattered—the shêkhs became rich landowners, while the tribesmen emerged in a totally different world as small-time farmers.

Transport and communications improved in the Fayoum with the railway connection to the Nile Valley in 1874, and the network of light railways throughout the province (a network that has since been pulled up). Baedeker noted in 1878 that Khedive Isma'îl "devotes special attention to this favoured part of his dominions." At one time, Isma'îl owned one-fifth of the cultivable land of Egypt, so it is hardly surprising that in the Fayoum "the railway between Medinet al-Fayoum and Abu Kesi [Abuksah] is used almost exclusively for the conveyance of sugar-cane to the manufactories of the Khedive."

The British, around the turn of the twentieth century, built good roads and revised the irrigation system. Land reclamation became possible. The Fayoum was finally recovering from the slump that had begun in Roman times.

Although most of Khedive Isma'îl's land was returned to the state in 1878, large-scale land ownership remained the norm until President Gamal 'Abd al-Nâṣir's land reforms of the 1950s, when farmers were finally able to own the land they had worked for generations, and escaped the yoke of the absentee Bey and Bâsha landlords that had been strangling their livelihood for so long. Since the 1950s, land reclamation, the establishment of cooperatives, and the rural electrification program, among other things, have led some way toward a revival of the prosperity the Fayoum once knew under the Ptolemies, though most of the land lost under the Romans remains desert still.

Traveling in the Fayoum

Early Travelers

The Fayoum, despite its remoteness, or perhaps because of it, has often been on the itinerary of visitors to Egypt, in both classical and modern times, and a number of interesting accounts of travel and observations in the province survive. The earliest and probably the best known is that of Herodotus, a Halicarnassian Greek, who visited the Fayoum in the course of his travels some time in the middle of the fifth century BCE and recorded his experiences in Book II of his *Histories*. During his guided tour, he was shown the Labyrinth at present-day Hawwâra, and Lake Moeris, ancestor of the modern Birkat Qarûn, and described both in awestruck detail. He also tells of the sacred crocodile, tamed and adorned with glass earrings and bracelets, fed on "bread, with a certain number of victims"; and of the veneration for crocodiles in general, mentioning in contrast the province of Elephantine, where crocodiles were actually hunted and eaten.

Strabo, another Greek, traveled widely in Egypt in the third decade BCE, that is, shortly after the country became a province of the Roman Empire, and over two hundred years after the Ptolemaic Greeks and Macedonians had first settled in the Fayoum. He was impressed by the fertility of the Fayoum, noting that it was the only part of Egypt to grow olive trees and produce olive oil. Wine was also produced, as well as grain, pulse, and other seed-plants. Strabo also saw and described the Labyrinth and Lake Moeris, and visited the sacred crocodile, whose diet had by this time changed to grain, pieces of meat, wine, and honey, "which are always being fed to it by the foreigners who go to see it." Reading Strabo's description of the feeding of the beast, one feels rather sorry for it, much as for a French force-fed goose: "When the priests went up to it, some of them opened its mouth, and another put in the cake, and again the meat, and then poured down the honey mixture. The animal then leaped into the lake and rushed across to the far side; but when another foreigner arrived, likewise carrying an offering of first-fruits, the priests took it, went around the lake in a run, took hold of the animal, and in the same manner fed it what it had been brought." It is surprising the poor creature had the agility to leap and rush at all! It seems that even if a crocodile was lucky enough to be free and wild, it ran the risk, while basking open-mouthed in the sun, of being killed in a most unfriendly manner by mongooses, which "throw themselves into [the crocodiles'] open jaws, eat through their entrails and bellies, and emerge from their dead bodies." Mongooses, of course, are still found in the Fayoum, but they chewed their way through their last crocodile a long time ago.

Modern European travelers and adventurers began to explore the Middle East in the seventeenth century. When M. Paul Lenoir visited the Fayoum in the late nineteenth century, his main object seems to have been to meet and fraternize with the dancing-girls of a certain quarter of old Sinnûris, but most early visitors came to see the antiquities, particularly those described by Herodotus and Strabo. The Labyrinth was a major attraction (although some travelers thought they had found its remains in the Ptolemaic temple of Qaṣr Qarûn), and so was the famous Lake Moeris. Other sights were taken in, and many casual observations from these early writings reveal something of the life of the Fayoum two or three hundred years ago. Paul Lucas, a French herbalist traveling in 1714, having in mind Herodotus' account of two pyramids in the middle of Lake Moeris, each surmounted by the seated figure of a king, desired to cross the lake to Golden Horn Island, expecting to find some remains there, but changed his mind when he saw the state of the fishing boats that were to ferry him across, and learned that the fishermen were afraid of sinking in the slightest wind.

Richard Pococke, an Englishman writing in 1743, gives an indication of the norms of female dress when he notes that while passing through Ṭubhâr (about twelve kilometers west of Fayoum), he saw "a young woman sitting by the road unveil'd, which was a certain sign of the profession she lived by." So veils were the norm then. When I lived in the Fayoum in the early 1980s, veils were worn only among the urban middle classes, never by country women; but in the 1990s things changed again, and most village women have now adopted the formerly urban *ḥigâb* in preference to the traditional headscarf, and some wear the full face-covering *niqâb*.

Before the building of the railway, the Fayoum was practically inaccessible in the high Nile season (late summer to fall), so visits were usually undertaken in winter, when the three-day journey from Cairo, either independently or with the weekly caravan, was relatively easy. Expeditions had to be well prepared, and this usually included (quite apart from arranging for camels, horses, tents, and provisions) securing the patronage of some important person in Cairo who could write letters of introduction and whose name would guarantee safe passage and assistance along the way. Bedouin raids from the desert were a danger, and a foreigner also had to be wary of getting caught up in the eternal running feuds between rival tribes. The Bedouin, however, while ruthless with their enemies, had very proud customs of hospitality. Once recognized as a guest in the camp or territory of a certain tribe, travelers enjoyed the ultimate protection and generosity of their host.

In January 1801, a French engineer with Bonaparte's invasion force, Dr. P. D. Martin, undertook an epic journey around the Birka. He first won the trust of Bedouin who, barely a year before, had been the bitterest enemies of the French, and then, under their protection, the only Frenchman with thirty Bedouin horsemen, rode into the remote desert north of the Birka, risking attack from rival tribes. The journey went off successfully, despite a warning, when they were approaching Qaṣr Qarûn, that enemy horsemen were in the area and had brutally murdered eight members of the escort tribe. Dr. Martin returned to a triumphal welcome at Minyat al-Ḥêṭ, seat of the head of the tribe, Shêkh Abu Ṣâliḥ. One of the most dramatic moments of the trip was the first sight of green land after two days in the desert:

> For 48 hours my eagerly searching eyes, constantly running over everything that was around me, had lighted on nothing but rocks and sand; only the image of death painted itself on my imagination, though without ever giving me the slightest impression of sadness or discomfort . . . but at the thrill afforded me by the first sight of greenery and living nature, I felt that, without my knowing it, my body had been in a continuous state of tension.

By the time he returned to Fayoum, Dr. Martin had spent four days on horseback and covered 150 kilometers on a round trip that had taken him to Biahmu, Sinnûris, Dimêh al-Sibâ‘, Qaṣr Qarûn, al-Nazla, Abu Gandîr, Madînat Mâḍi, al-Gharaq, and Minyat al-Ḥêṭ and had brought him so close to his companions that he was hailed as a member of their tribe. Dr. Martin wrote a fascinating account of his adventures in Bonaparte's great catalog, the *Description de l'Egypte*, but the end of his tale is rather sad. Having become attached to the Fayoum and his Bedouin friends, he hoped to remain there in his capacity as engineer to carry out some much-needed repair and maintenance work on the irrigation system, but he was recalled to work on a road in Damietta. Still determined to see the Fayoum again, he obtained permission to return later in the year, but before he had a chance to do so the British arrived, and the entire French presence, including Dr. Martin, had to disappear rather rapidly. He never did see Egypt or the Fayoum again.

Traveling in the Fayoum Today

Being a Foreigner

When traveling around Egypt outside Cairo, unless you can pass for an Egyptian, you must accept being an object of attention and curiosity nearly everywhere you go, and this certainly applies in the Fayoum. Your appearance, dress, behavior, and the way you speak are all strange and often entertaining. It should be remembered that the attention you generate is very rarely hostile (the Egyptians are the friendliest people in the world), but it can occasionally be so if you appear to break social customs of dress and behavior. If you want to have a relaxing, enjoyable holiday and experience the real warmth and hospitality of the Fayoumis, there are a few things it is worth bearing in mind.

Both men and women should avoid showing too much skin. Women should wear clothes that cover the shoulders, and the legs down to the knees. Women with long hair, particularly if it is blonde, may feel more comfortable if they put it up or cover it with a headscarf. Men should never remove their shirts, and should also not uncover their shoulders or any part of the legs. An Australian visitor once went off in a service taxi to the Birka wearing T-shirt and shorts, and came back wondering why an old woman in the taxi had kept touching his legs and laughing. The answer was, simply, the shorts–in Egyptian eyes, he was wandering around in his underwear. Long hair in men is usually ridiculed. Generally speaking, a tidy, well-groomed appearance goes a long way to establishing good relations.

Public displays of affection between the sexes are extremely rare in rural and small-town Egypt. Holding hands or linking arms is acceptable, although people will assume you are engaged or married. Anything more intimate will give offense.

Queues are almost always double–one for men, one for women. If you automatically pick the shorter one, you may find yourself in with the wrong sex and the cause of some agitation.

There are a few other social customs that might be taken note of, to avoid confusion or embarrassment. If you too fervently express admiration for someone's personal property, you may soon find the object, no matter how valuable to the owner, being pressed upon you as a gift. This can sometimes be quite difficult to refuse. Admiration of children by strangers is very strictly taboo. The child is not likely to be offered to you, but the parent may become quite upset. This is connected with the belief, particularly strong among the farming population, in the frightening curse of the Evil Eye, which, if attracted by envy to a possession or a person may do material harm.

Men are expected to smoke, women are not. If you are unlucky enough to be a man who does not smoke, you may find yourself spending a lot of time trying to refuse cigarettes. Offers and invitations are governed by a complex ritual of repeating the offer and repeatedly refusing it. If you really want someone to accept your offer of a biscuit or cup of tea, you may have to insist three or four or more times. Similarly, if you really want to refuse that *fûl* sandwich or Pepsi-Cola, you may have to do so an equal number of times. If you want to accept an offer it is polite to refuse initially at least once. There is a species of offer or invitation, known in Arabic as a 'boatman's invitation,' which is never intended to be accepted, but is made as a polite gesture, and a single refusal is usually sufficient. The boatman's invitation, so called from the invitations called out from swiftly-passing boats to friends on the bank, may be encountered when your neighbor on the bus offers you his only sandwich or his last cigarette, or, on leaving the bus, invites you home, though he knows you are traveling on to the next town or village. A similar phenomenon may be experienced in shops or cafés when you are invited to keep the money you offer in payment. This is again a gesture of politeness or friendliness, and should never be accepted—you must insist on paying.

Water is considered a gift of God, and is therefore never seen as private property. This means that you can ask anybody for water, as long as it is available. Conversely, if you are carrying water, you should give it to anybody who asks for it.

There are a hundred thousand other ways in which Egyptian habits and customs differ from western ones, particularly in rural areas like the Fayoum. Those outlined above are just a few of the more important points that may arise. Others can be noted by an observant eye. Perhaps the final point to note, from which you may derive some comfort, is that Egyptians normally make generous allowances for the peculiar behavior of foreign visitors, and treat them as honored guests despite breaches of etiquette.

A Note on Photography

Egyptians enjoy being photographed, but only if they are ready for you. Photography is something that has to be handled sensitively. If anybody really objects to being photographed, which is very rare, it is as well to give in, smile, and put your camera away. People you photograph often ask for copies of the pictures. This is up to you, but it is sometimes a small price to pay for a good shot.

Sometimes you may be prevented from photographing a street or village scene that you may see as attractive, but which an Egyptian sees as dirty and bringing shame on the country. Again, don't insist: give way. Photography of military installations, bridges, and certain buildings is illegal, and if you try it, or even if you do it accidentally, you may have your film or memory card confiscated.

Approaches and Transport to the Fayoum

Three main roads enter the Fayoum: one from Cairo and Gîza in the northeast; one from al-Wâsṭa in the east; and one from Beni Swêf in the southeast. There are pyramids along each. The Cairo road passes the Gîza pyramids, and later, just after a railway line in the desert, there is often a good view of the Dahshûr pyramids on the horizon to the left. The al-Wâsṭa road skirts close by Maydûm pyramid just after leaving the Nile Valley, and Hawwâra pyramid just before entering the Fayoum. The Beni Swêf road passes al-Lahûn and Hawwâra pyramids, both on the right. Both the al-Wâsṭa and Beni Swêf roads can now be reached via the new desert road to Asyûṭ, which leaves the Cairo–Fayoum road 20 kilometers south of the Gîza pyramids and cuts through the desert between the Fayoum and the Nile Valley.

The *Cairo road* leaves Gîza at the very end of Pyramids Street, with a right turn at the foot of the hill leading to the pyramids themselves, then a left turn at the traffic circle in front of the Meridien Pyramids Hotel. It is then some 80 kilometers to the obelisk (al-Misalla) at the entrance to Fayoum city. The first 50 kilometers are across bare desert, much of it with excellent views back to the pyramids of Gîza. There is a toll booth (current toll LE3) after 40 kilometers, then a police checkpoint 10 kilometers farther on. With the Kôm Ôshîm Museum and ruins of Karanis on your left, you reach the real rim of the basin 5 kilometers later and drop down into rich green land that was once the lake bed. Another 2 kilometers take you to the turnoff right to the lake and Wâdi al-Rayyân, while the main road continues southward to Fayoum, bypassing Sinnûris and other villages on the way.

The *Beni Swêf road* leaves the west of the town and strikes north, reaching Fayoum in 40 kilometers. The Baḥr Yûsuf is crossed at al-Lahûn, 22 kilometers from Beni Swêf, then the road follows the right bank of a branch canal, the Baḥr Ḥasan Wâṣif, for about 12 kilometers along the southern edge of the narrow Lahûn Gap. After passing al-'Azab monastery on the left, the road leaves the canal and soon turns north to enter Fayoum in the south at al-Ḥawâtim.

The *al-Wâsṭa road* turns west off the main Nile Valley road just north of the small town of al-Wâsṭa, and soon enters the desert, which is mostly very flat. The road crosses the railway, then reaches and parallels newly reclaimed land on the right for some time, with military installations on the left. Just before Hawwâra pyramid, a right turn takes the route to and through the village of Demu, across Maṣraf al-Baṭs (a rocky valley with a stream), to meet the railway again. A left turn here leads into the eastern end of Fayoum, about 40 kilometers from al-Wâsṭa.

Trains to Fayoum from Ramsis station in Cairo go the long way around, via al-Wâsṭa, and take about four hours.

The best form of public transport from Cairo to Fayoum are the air-conditioned *buses* that leave at frequent intervals from 6:00am to 6:00pm from 'Abbûd in Shubra. Seats can be booked in advance, to a maximum of two days. Often it is possible to arrive and find seats on the next bus, but if you want to travel on a Thursday after mid-morning be sure to book at least half a day ahead, as this is the start of the weekend for a large number of Fayoumis working or studying in Cairo. Apart from the air-conditioned buses, there are other cheaper, more crowded, less comfortable buses leaving from both 'Abbûd and Munîb (under the bridge) south of Gîza Station. The journey from Cairo to Fayoum usually takes about two hours. Buses leave Fayoum (from under the bridge that crosses the railway line on the eastern outskirts of town, 2E2) for Cairo at the same regular intervals, and, as at 'Abbûd, seats can be booked in advance.

The third form of public transport from Cairo to Fayoum is the *service taxi:* either Peugeot seven-seater station wagons or fifteen-seater 'microbuses,' which leave from the same place as the buses in Munîb, at most times of the day and night. The driver sets off as soon as all the seats are filled, and usually reaches Fayoum in well under an hour and a half. Traveling in these taxis is much safer than it used to be, since the completion of the divided highway all the way to Fayoum, but they can still be fast and dangerous, and those of a nervous disposition should avoid them. On reaching Fayoum, both buses and taxis may let you out in town near the Baḥr Yûsuf, but their final destination is the terminal under the bridge—and this is where you have to get to when you want to catch a bus or taxi back to Cairo.

Arriving *from Upper Egypt* by train, get off at Beni Swêf, cross the railway tracks and the canal behind them, and turn south: about 500 meters along the road on the right you will find the taxis to Fayoum near the bus station. Like the Gîza ones, they are the fill-up-and-go type. They arrive in Fayoum at al-Ḥawâtim, in the south of the town, and this is where they leave from again for Beni Swêf. If you want to get from Fayoum to Beni Swêf in time for a train, you should allow at least two hours from al-Ḥawâtim, as there may be a long wait for the taxi to fill up.

Traveling within the Fayoum

Although Fayoum city has grown in the last twenty years, it is still true that most journeys can be made on foot, and the center can be reached from most parts of the town in ten or fifteen minutes. There are still horse-cabs *(ḥanṭûr/ḥanaṭîr)* for hire, but there are now also taxis, with a fixed fare (currently LE2) anywhere within the city, and there are microbuses that follow numbered routes.

For getting out of town and around the Fayoum, there are four main types of public transport.

Service taxis (servîs) constitute the most wide-ranging and convenient form of public transport and almost every village is connected by them to Fayoum, either directly or indirectly. Service taxis have fixed starting and finishing points, fixed routes, and fixed fares for stages along their routes. In this respect, they are much like a bus service. Where they differ is in not running to a timetable, but in setting off as soon as they are full, after which the next driver in the line immediately starts to fill his car. Fares are usually collected by a small boy hanging on to the outside of the car. No tickets are given.

The supply/demand balance of service taxis varies greatly with the route, the time of the day, and the day of the week. Sometimes there are too many people and not enough taxis, in which case it is difficult to get a ride; at other times there are not enough people and you can sit in a taxi for half an hour or more before it fills up. Usually, though, the service is quite quick, efficient, and reliable. The stations for service taxis are moved so frequently and so drastically from one site to another that there seems little point in me telling you where they currently are: just ask anybody to direct you (or get a taxi to take you) to *maw·af* ——, putting the name of the village you want to go to in the blank. At the station, ask for the name of the place you want, and you will be shown to a car. Often, when returning to Fayoum from somewhere other than a village center, you will need to wait by the roadside and flag down any passing taxi. If it has room it will stop.

Taxis can be hired in Fayoum to take you out of town. Your route and price must be negotiated with the driver.

Tuk-tuks (three-wheeled motorbikes with covered cabins, flashing lights, and erratic and often underage drivers) operate in, around, and among the villages, on a private-hire basis.

Motorbike taxis are found in some of the larger villages, and at several points around Fayoum, including near the Misalla. They take up to three passengers, and as a last resort are worth considering.

Fayoum City

مدينة الفيوم ▪ *madînat al-fayyûm*

The main town of the Fayoum is not, as some guidebooks would have it, usually known as al-Medîna. As Maṣr, for many, means both Egypt and Cairo, so al-Fayoum is both the province and its capital. For convenience in English we may refer to the former as the Fayoum, the latter as Fayoum.

Baedeker's 1878 guide to Egypt described Fayoum as a "not unpleasing specimen of an Egyptian town," and that restrained Victorian double negative encapsulates perfectly the essential undemonstrative tone of the place. It is not an awe-inspiring beauty-spot and has no exceptional tourist attractions, but it is not ugly and exerts a subtle, friendly charm on people with the time to spare to take it in.

The town is sited on high land (about 22 meters above sea level, and about 8 meters below the level of the Nile at Beni Swêf) in the southeast of the Fayoum depression, on both banks of the Baḥr Yûsuf at the point where it ends its meandering 300-kilometer journey from Dayrût and radiates in eight main distributary canals. The gently curving course of the canalized river, with its numerous low, flat bridges, forms the central focus and orientation of the town. Everything seems to gravitate to al-Baḥr, as it is familiarly called, and this is particularly apparent on summer evenings when the young people of the town walk up and down one bank or the other, meet, talk, lean on the bridges, sit on the walls and watch the passers-by, very much in the manner of an Italian *corso*. During the day, hand-carts, donkey-carts, horse-cabs, bicycles, motorbikes, cars, taxis, minibuses, vans, and trucks compete with pedestrians on the roads and bridges.

The town has stood on its present site at least since the thirteenth century when Abu 'Uthmân al-Nabulsi was governor. In his *History of the Fayoum and its Towns*, written in 1245, he noted that Fayoum, three days' journey from Fustâṭ, was built on both banks of the Baḥr Yûsuf, as now. Each half of the town had its bazaars, and the whole town was surrounded by magnificent orchards and gardens of great fecundity, producing fruits of all kinds, jasmine, and the exquisite roses for which the Fayoum was widely famed. The town must then have been protected by city walls that have since disappeared, as one of the four churches mentioned, Archangel Michael, is said to stand "near the S[inn]ûris gate," while another, the Virgin Mary, stood "outside the walls." Twenty-three mosques are enumerated, including a congregational mosque *(gami')* built on a bridge of four arches. This building, the mosque of Ibn Faḥl, has been said to be the forerunner of the fifteenth-century mosque of Qaytbay (see page 44), the four arches of the bridge having been reduced at some stage to the present two.

Dr. Martin, visiting Fayoum at the beginning of 1801, mentions a Nuweiri Gate, implying that the city walls still stood, at least in part. He also informs us that the Baḥr Sinnûris and Baḥr Tersa left the Baḥr Yûsuf at the very eastern end of town, indicating that the town has since grown considerably eastward and that the old center was in what is now the western part of the city.

In earlier times, from the Old Kingdom at least until the Roman period, the main town of the region stood at Kimân Fâris (see page 42), slightly to the north of modern Fayoum. Diodorus records the ancient legend that Crocodilopolis (Fayoum) was originally built by the semi-mythical King Menes, uniter of Upper and Lower Egypt, after his life was saved by a crocodile on the Great Lake. Modern Fayoumis have their own legend about the origins of their city. They say it was built in a period of a thousand days and was consequently romantically named 'City of a Thousand Days'–Madînat Elf Yôm, which was then corrupted to Madînat al-Fayoum. Like most other folk etymologies, it is a lovely story, but unfortunately rather a long way from the more prosaic truth. Fayoum, originally the name of the province, later applied to its main town, is derived from the Bohairic Coptic *fa-yom*, 'the sea.'

Places to Stay

Fortunately it is no longer true that "quarters for the night may be procured at the house of the Italian curé . . . but not elsewhere without difficulty" (Baedeker 1878). Apart from the numerous cheap and rough hotels all over town, there are a few mid-range hotels, including the Montazah (2C2; tel: 084 634-8662) and the Queen (2D2; tel: 084 634-6819), both in Menshât Luṭfallah. The Faculty of Tourism and Hotels of Fayoum University runs its own training hotel in the university grounds at Kimân Fâris; entrance is from the main street just beyond the ship-shaped mosque. The hotel is also ship-shape: smart, clean, and well-run with friendly service (off 2C2; tel: 084 634-5702; fax: 084 635-6631).

Outside the town, the Auberge Hotel (1D1; tel: 084 698-1200; fax: 084 698-1300; auberge@helnan.com; www.helnan.com) and the very attractive Panorama Hotel (1D2; tel & fax: 084 683-0757 or 683-0746 or 683-0314) are situated on the Birka, while there are chalets at 'În al-Siliyîn (1D2; tel: 010 196-1042).

Places to Eat

Eating in Fayoum, as in most other Egyptian towns, is hardly ever a problem, and there are places to please all palates and all pockets.

The best *kushari* in town is still served at Sa'îd, on the Baḥr Sinnûris where it leaves the Baḥr Yûsuf (2D3)—a bowl of macaroni, spaghetti, rice, lentils, chickpeas, and fried onions, with the option of a hot pepper sauce, costs next to nothing. The odd shape of this little restaurant and the rushing water of the Baḥr Sinnûris sluice alongside almost give the impression of eating on a boat.

There are a number of clean and convenient fast-food-style eating places along Nâdi Street (2C2), such as Kalbaz and Yamâl al-Shâm, and on al-Daḥdûra (2C3), like al-Khidîwi.

For good and filling food, try the Governorate Club *(nâdi al-muḥâfza)*, in the north of the town (2D1). At the back of the building is a pleasant garden, where you can eat under the trees and watch the ducks and geese on the Baḥr Sinnûris.

Outside the town, on the Birka, the Auberge Hotel (1D1) has a plush dining room, the Panorama Hotel (1D2) serves good food on an attractive bougainvillea-clad terrace, and Cafeteria Gebel al-Zîna (1D1) serves excellent fish in more modest surroundings. East of the Auberge, the Lu·lu·a (1D1) serves a good lunch under a wooden lattice canopy on an artificial promontory in the lake.

Entertainment

Fayoum has two cinemas, which are usually crowded and always noisy, and films are very difficult to follow. The new Palace of Culture (the extraordinary upside-down pyramid in the center of town 2D3) hosts theater, music, and films, and Fayoum now has its very own zoo, next to the Governorate building in the north of the town (2E1). But the main source of entertainment is the cafés, which, though considered by many middle-class Fayoumis as being beneath their dignity, abound in all parts of the town and are well attended. The cafés are generally male territory, but Fayoumis make generous allowances for the strange behavior of foreigners and do not mind foreign women sitting in their cafés. The cafés vary greatly in size, style, and range of drinks served, but all serve tea *(shây)* and coffee *(·ahwa*, served with sugar *mazbûṭ*, with a touch of sugar *'arrîḥa*, with a lot of sugar *ziyâda*, or with no sugar at all *sâda)*. Others may serve cold, fizzy, bottled drinks, or other hot drinks like fenugreek *(ḥelba)*, cocoa *(kakâw)*, cinnamon *(·irfa)*, salep *(saḥlab)*, ginger *(ganzabîl)*, hibiscus *(kerkadêh)*, and aniseed *(yansûn)*. Water-pipes *(shîsha* or *bûri)* are served in all cafés. Dominos are often played in the cafés, occasionally chess, but the favorite game is backgammon *(ṭâwla)*. Various versions of backgammon are played, though the object of all seems to be the same—to make more noise than your partner in slapping down the plastic counters on the wooden box-board. The favorite is *maḥbûsa* ('prisoner'), in which, to delay your opponent's progress around the board, you attempt to trap and hold prisoner his counters. Others are *gilbahâr, wâḥid wa talatîn* ('thirty-one'), *'âda* ('ordinary,' the game understood as backgammon in the west), and a child's game, *yahûdi* ('Jewish'). Backgammon boards are charged for in some cafés, in others not.

The Obelisk of Abgîg مسلة أبجيج ▪ *misallat abgîg*

As you enter the town from Cairo, you pass a large monument of red granite in the middle of a traffic circle (2E1). Actually a stela, not an obelisk, it was erected by Senwosret I (second king of the Twelfth Dynasty and founder of the famous obelisk of Heliopolis), though its decoration and inscriptions are much worn down and difficult to make out. It was still standing at its original site near Abgîg (1D3), a small village on the road to Iṭsa, when Richard Pococke visited the Fayoum in the 1740s, but sixty years later a French artist, Jomard, recording monuments for the *Description de l'Egypte*, found it lying on the ground, broken in two, and thus it remained until the 1970s, when the great stone, weighing altogether 100 tons, was painstakingly transported, reconstructed, and erected on its present site by the local Department of Antiquities. It now stands about 13 meters high. For a good impression of how the stela looked lying broken in the fields outside Abgîg, see figure 58 in E. W. Lane's *Description of Egypt.*

Kimân Fâris كيمان فارس ▪ 'Mounds of Fâris'

Out to the north of the city is the almost totally built-over site of the ancient capital of the Fayoum, Shedet/Crocodilopolis/Arsinoë (2C1). Baedeker's 1929 guide speaks of "one of the most extensive ruins of any old Egyptian town," and there was still a vast area of broken pottery littered with a few statues and broken columns when I arrived in Fayoum in 1979, but now hardly anything remains to view. If you are determined enough you can see the few sorry fragments, fenced off among—and sometimes in the grounds of—the various university faculties that now occupy most of the site, but frankly it is no longer worth it. Many fascinating small artifacts discovered at Kimân Fâris during building operations are now displayed in the Kôm Ôshîm Museum.

The Seven Waterwheels السبع سواقى ■ *al-saba' sawâ·i*

The symbol of the Fayoum Governorate is the large, black waterwheel that is peculiar to the province. The Fayoum's waterwheels are not only unique, but also quite beautiful. Big, solid, shiny black, with crystal-clear water gushing from them (even in the dirtiest of streams), their great axles whining and moaning and groaning with hypnotic effect, they are the most marvelous of machines. Their uniqueness lies in the fact that they are driven by the stream itself—the power of the water pushes round the large paddles, while the boxes in the rim fill with water, lift it up, and spill it out of the holes in their sides when they reach the top, into a channel that leads the water off to the fields. The wheels run continuously, but if water is not required the opening of a sluice sends it back into the main stream. The practicability of water-driven wheels in the Fayoum is mostly due to the gradient of the land (from 26 meters above sea level in the southeast to 45 below in the north) and the consequent abundance of fast-flowing streams, as opposed to the sluggish canals of Upper Egypt and the Delta; and to the ingenuity of Ptolemaic engineers, who first introduced the wheels as part of the general drive to develop agriculture in the Fayoum in the third century BCE.

The wheels are said to number about two hundred throughout the province. They are usually between 4 and 5 meters in diameter, and are capable of lifting water to a maximum of 3 meters. Tarring gives them their color and protects them from decay. Repairs are most easily carried out in January, when the canals are dry and the wheels stop and become white with dead algae. If repairs are needed at other times of the year, the wheels must be stopped by hand, a feat that requires the strength of half a dozen men.

The Seven Waterwheels (currently only six, though it is to be hoped that the missing one will be replaced soon) are situated picturesquely on the Baḥr Sinnûris, a half-hour walk out of the town (2D1). Follow the Baḥr Sinnûris, first on its west bank then on its east, northward out of town, behind the Governorate Club, into the country. A short way down the canal is a single wheel at a farm; a little farther on is a beautiful group of four, backed by rich mango trees, tall palms, and classic weeping willows; and a little farther still is the final pair, with a rough bridge. Quite apart from the attraction of the waterwheels, this is a delightful country walk, especially in the early morning or just before sunset.

The waterwheels can now also be reached from the Cairo Road: coming from Cairo by car, turn right on the Ring Road, then after 1 kilometer turn left (*not* right, as per the signpost) to arrive at the wheels in the reverse order to that described above.

Old Mosques

Fayoumis are not as used as Cairenes to foreigners entering and looking around their mosques, so it is probably best to limit your interest to the three historic mosques listed below, and here, although no entrance fee is charged, you should ask permission of the guardian of the mosque before entering and again before taking any photographs. Avoid the main prayer-times (dawn, noon, mid-afternoon, sunset, an hour and a half after sunset) and dress appropriately, otherwise you may be turned away. For men, long trousers and a short-sleeved shirt are acceptable; for women, shoulders and arms should be covered, and a dress should reach at least to the knees. Bare shoulders and legs, of either sex, would be particularly offensive in a mosque. Remember to take off your shoes and leave them outside.

The Hanging Mosque (المسجد المعلق • *al-masgid al-mu'allaq*) is found up a small side street to the north off the Baḥr Yûsuf, just past the fourth bridge west of the town-center waterwheels (2C3). A flight of broken steps leads up to the back (south) of the mosque. At the front (north) at ground level are five arches, which once each housed an artisan's workshop. The mosque is built over these (hence the name), and a double flight of steps leads up to the main doorway, which is decorated with carved Quranic inscriptions. The mosque has undergone extensive reconstruction, though the basic shell of limestone blocks, with its iron-grille windows, remains.

The Mosque of Qaytbây (مسجد قايتباى • *masgid qaytbây*) stands on the south bank of the Baḥr Yûsuf, by the sixth bridge west of the waterwheels (2B3). The Circassian Mamluk sultan al-Ashraf Sayf al-Dîn Qaytbây, renowned warrior, torturer, and builder, who ruled Egypt from 1468 to 1496, made occasional visits to the Fayoum, including one in March 1476 when he came especially to see the newly-completed orchard and watermill of one of his ministers, Khayrbak Ḥadîd, on his Fayoum estate. It was probably on this visit that Qaytbây began work on the mosque that bears his name. It is usually assumed that he built the mosque and the bridge by which it stands, but it has been suggested that he merely restored the existing mosque of Ibn Faḥl, mentioned by Nabulsi in the thirteenth century, and that the bridge was also an earlier work. The bridge is a solid but attractive two-arched construction, formerly named for Qaytbây's wife, Khwand Aṣl Bây (in whose honor it is said he built the mosque), but now more usually known by the poignant name Qanṭarat Bâb al-Widâ' (Bridge of the Gate of Farewells) because it leads to the cemetery.

The main door of the mosque is on the south side and is very fine. Set in a large recess in the heavy stone wall, decorated with carved blocks of Quranic texts, the double door is of heavy wood, beautifully ornamented with now green bronze. Inside, many of the columns are clearly ancient (some have Corinthian capitals) and were probably taken from the ruins of Arsinoë at Kimân Fâris, a short distance to the north. To the left as you enter is a curtained-off section for women, and just near this under one of the mats is a well in the floor, originally used for raising water for ablutions. The well has a direct connection with the Baḥr Yûsuf. On the eastern wall, to the left of the large, rather plain *miḥrâb* (prayer-niche), is a small plaque giving details of the building of the mosque. The large *minbar* (pulpit) is an excellent example of Islamic decorative art—intricately carved wood with inlaid ivory from Somalia. The Quran bench next to the minbar is also well executed.

The Mausoleum of 'Ali al-Rûbi (قبة مسجد على الروبى • *·ubbat masgid 'ali al-rûbi*) is close to the Mosque of Qaytbây (2B3). Follow the Baḥr Yûsuf back toward town a short way and before the next bridge turn right up a narrow street, opposite a mosque on the far bank of the river. When the street opens out, you will see to your right the dome and minaret of the 'Ali al-Rûbi mosque, and the large entrance leading into a covered courtyard. At the far right-hand corner of the courtyard, down some steps, is the door to the mausoleum of 'Ali al-Rûbi. The interior appears small and cramped because of the size of the *ḍarîḥ*, the carved box-frame surrounding and screening the tomb. The dome above is large and light, but plain. The tomb of Shêkh 'Ali al-Rûbi, the favorite local holy man, is particularly revered by many Fayoumis, who come here with special prayers and supplications, which they mutter or chant or shout while walking around the *ḍarîḥ*. The mosque is also the focus of one of the Fayoum's most popular religious festivals (see below).

Religious Festivals

All Islamic festivals move forward in relation to the western solar calendar by about ten days each year. Below is the list of the Islamic months, with corresponding starting dates for 2009—allow for a variation of a day or two.

A.H. 1430	I	Muḥarram	(2008) December 29
	II	Ṣafar	(2009) January 27
	III	Rabî' al-Awwal	February 26
	IV	Rabî' al-Tâni	March 28
	V	Gamâda al-Ûla	April 26
	VI	Gamâda al-Ukhra	May 26
	VII	Ragab	June 24
	VIII	Sha'bân	July 23
	IX	Ramaḍân	August 21
	X	Shawwâl	September 20
	XI	Dhû al-Qa'da	October 19
	XII	Dhû al-Ḥigga	November 18
A.H. 1431	I	Muḥarram	December 18

Around the middle of Sha'bân is celebrated the *mûlid* (birthday festival) of *'Ali al-Rûbi*, one of the most important *mûlids* in the area. For several days, people converge from all parts of the Fayoum, as well as from Beni Swêf and farther afield, on the area around the saint's tomb (see above) to celebrate, in both spiritual and secular ways, the birthday of the great shêkh. The hotels overflow, and many people sleep in the streets.

The streets and alleys around the mosque are lined with stalls and sideshows, and thronged with excited masses caught up in the fun-fair atmosphere. The stalls sell a variety of very sweet sweets, and everything is brightly colored—the tenting around the sweet stalls and temporary cafés; the air-rifle target-practice sideshows, where you aim at little cap-bombs from nearly point-blank range; the try-your-strength battering-rams on ascending tracks; the children's boat-swings. And everything is noisy.

In the courtyard of the mosque, the more spiritual side of the celebrations take place. Here, to rhythmic music and chanting, men perform the *zikr*, standing in lines in front of the musicians, swinging their heads over first one shoulder then the other in time to the beating of the drums, hoping to fall into a trance, while watched and willed on by a buzzing crowd. The participants consider themselves particularly well blessed if they collapse in a faint, as they believe this brings them into a closer communion with God.

The *Prophet's Birthday* (مولد النبى • *mûlid al-nabi*), on the twelfth day of Rabî' al-Awwal, tends to be celebrated more soberly, with a national holiday and a visit to the mosque, though stalls of sweets of the kind described above do appear on the streets.

Another large *mûlid* is held during Ramaḍân in honor of *Shêkha Maryam*, a holy woman whose small, white-domed tomb can be seen on the north side of the Baḥr Yûsuf between the Baḥr Sinnûris sluice and the waterwheels.

Apart from these major *mûlids*, almost every village in the Fayoum has its own special one at a fixed point in the Islamic calendar, in memory of its particular local shêkh, and you may come across one of these any time by accident.

A large, colorful procession to mark the beginning of Ramaḍân takes place in Fayoum in the late afternoon on the last day of Sha'bân (just before the first of Ramaḍân begins at sunset). This is called الرؤية • *al-Ru·ya*, which means literally 'the sighting' and refers to the sighting of the new moon, which heralds the start of the holiest of Islamic months. A couple of hours before sunset, at the Gamal 'Abd al-Nâṣir mosque (2E3), the Governor of the Fayoum makes a speech, which is relayed by loudspeaker to the large, excited crowds waiting along the route of the procession. The procession then starts from the mosque, passes the railway station, skirts behind the waterwheels, and crosses the canal. Meanwhile all intersecting roads are completely blocked and nothing moves in or out of the city until the procession is past.

The police and security forces head the march, then come the Ṣûfi orders, carrying religious banners and flags. The larger part of the parade is made up of carnival floats belonging to various trade guilds—bakers, carpenters, etc.—decorated after the theme of the trade, and usually manned by a good number of its practitioners energetically, and often comically, demonstrating or miming their skills. Every now and then someone on a float or in the crowd tosses a handful of leaflets into the air, which sets off a good-natured battle among the spectators to win one of these valuable prizes—calendars of the month of Ramaḍân, bearing the name of a local store or firm for advertising: they give details of all the prayer times and exactly what time the fast begins and ends each day.

As the procession passes, the crowds disperse, traffic starts to move again, and thus begins *Ramaḍân*. The following thirty days reveal a city at half-steam in the daytime and more than full-steam at night. At sunset, when nearly everybody is at home for the first taste of food and water since before sunrise, Fayoum is like a ghost town, but within an hour the streets become busier than ever and remain so for most of the night. Many people do not sleep until dawn. During the day, stores and offices work short hours, fasters take it easy, and the pace of business and life in general shifts into low gear. Fasting often makes tempers short, but while more fights occur on hot Ramaḍân afternoons than at any other time of the year, probably as many are avoided with a well-timed "May every year see you well," the seasonal greeting: a gentle reminder that it is Ramaḍân and that everybody is in the same waterless boat.

At the end of Ramaḍân, a three-day holiday marks the *Little Feast* (العيد الصغير • *al-'îd al-ṣughayyar*), celebrated with the same kind of cookies and small cakes that the Christian community make for Christmas (which also marks the end of a long fast, though of a different kind).

Two months and ten days later, starting on the tenth of Dhû al-Ḥigga, comes the *Great Feast* (العيد الكبير • *al-'îd al-kibîr*), which entails a holiday of four days, during which everything stops, and stores and restaurants close. This is the only time of year when it might be difficult to find anything to eat. The feast celebrates the slaughter of the ram by Ibrahîm (Abraham) in place of his son Isma'îl (Ishmael, not Isaac as in the Bible), and any family that can afford it slaughters its own sheep, giving a portion of the meat to the poor. Other families buy pieces of lamb from the butcher. The scale of the butchers' business on the morning of the Feast, judged by the pools of blood in the streets, has to be seen (though not by the squeamish) to be believed. The other tradesman kept busy in the days before the Feast is the itinerant knifegrinder with his portable grindstone.

The one major festival and holiday observed by both Muslims and Christians in the Fayoum, as in the rest of Egypt, is *Shamm al-Nesîm* (شم النسيم • , 'smelling the breeze'), an ancient Egyptian celebration of the end of winter and the coming of the summer breezes. It has no fixed date, always falling on the Monday after the highly mobile Coptic Easter. Shamm al-Nesîm is a holiday for most people, and Fayoumis like to get out into the countryside as early as possible for a family picnic and games. The two most popular venues, of course, are the Birka and 'În al-Siliyîn, and trippers from Cairo also come here, so both places become extremely crowded. The traditional foods of Shamm al-Nesîm are hard-boiled eggs, often with decorated shells, and salted fish *(mulûḥa* or *fisîkh)*. Also sold from temporary stalls along Baḥr Yûsuf are the bright paper hats *(ṭaraṭîr)* and children's games essential for a jolly Shamm al-Nesîm country outing.

Churches

There are several churches in the town, only one of which is of any historical interest. Note that although the Coptic Orthodox Church has its own liturgical calendar (the year 1725 began on September 11, 2008), its feasts are timed according to the Julian calendar, which falls thirteen days behind the Gregorian calendar. This means that fixed feasts such as Christmas (January 7) fall thirteen days later than they do in the west, while Easter, being movable and because of the complicated calculations involved, may sometimes be celebrated on the same Sunday as in the west, but may fall up to five weeks later.

The *Church of the Holy Virgin (*كنيسة العذراء • *kinîsat al-'adra)* is the oldest church in the city (2B3). The exact date of the building is not known, but a date appears on the altar-screen above the door to the sanctuary: ١٥٥٢, i.e., 1552 of the Coptic calendar, equivalent to 1836 CE. The renovation and paintings inside the church are recent: Christ, the four evangelists, and Melchizedek and Aaron (in the Old Testament, the heads of the two separate lines of High Priests) appear in the central dome. The altar-screen, running right along the eastern end of the church, completely hiding the altars and sanctuary from the congregation, is attractively decorated with dark and light wood inlays. In front of the altar-screen are two ivory-inlaid Bible-stands and the Bishop's throne, and above it hang two ostrich eggs, a common feature in Coptic churches: they are said to remind people that just as the ostrich stands at a distance continually watching and waiting for its eggs to hatch, so Christians must continually watch and wait for the Second Coming. Behind the altar-screen (remove your shoes), the sanctuary is divided into three parts. The central sanctuary, containing the main altar with its golden dome, is for priests only. The two side-sections are for men (north) and women (south) to come and take communion.

There is a second altar in the northern sanctuary dedicated to Anba Abrâm, the highly revered local saint. This is the white-bearded gentleman you see in many pictures around Fayoum's churches and monasteries. Anba Abrâm was born in 1829 in Dayrûṭ, Upper Egypt, and after entering the Muḥarraq Monastery near his home was appointed Bishop of the Fayoum and Gîza in 1882. He was a latter-day ascetic, possessing, it is said, only one cloak, and eschewing money and all material comforts—he never sat in chairs—and he became known in his own lifetime as a very holy man. Various miracles are associated with him, and he is said to have reached such a state of spiritual perfection that his body became 'fluid' and he could appear and disappear and transport himself across distances in miraculous fashion. The small building on the south side of the church was his residence, and a room has been set aside as a small museum and shrine to the saint, containing paintings, icons, and a collection of letters signed by him. He died in 1914.

Services are held in the church on Sundays, Wednesdays, and Fridays at 7am. The liturgy is in Coptic, while sermons are given in Arabic. To reach the Church of the Holy Virgin, follow the directions given for the gold market (see following section), but instead of turning sharp left at the twist in the street by the minaret, carry on in the same direction past the mosque to find the church about 100 meters farther on.

The *Sûq*

Like any other Egyptian town, Fayoum has its *sûq*, the traditional, old-style trading area, where all manner of goods, produce, and crafts are bargained and haggled over in the crowded narrow streets (2C3). This area in Fayoum is known as al-Qanṭara *(al-·anṭara)*, and is most easily entered by a narrow, covered street running diagonally to the Baḥr Yûsuf, at the point where it is covered by an extended bridge (the fourth bridge west of the waterwheels). A wander around al-Qanṭara is always interesting, but be warned that the place is labyrinthine and it is easier to find your way in than out. It is not a large area, but the streets are narrow, twisting, and irregular and meet and diverge at strange angles. Dead ends are common, but if you stay with the crowds, you should not get too seriously lost.

Some of the streets are covered in medieval style by slatted wood or sagging sheets of cloth, keeping out the hot sun and at the same time filling the streets with a soft, dusty, diffused light that enhances the timeless atmosphere. Most parts of the *sûq* are devoted to one particular trade or product. This is the traditional system of commerce in the Middle East, where artisans or sellers of a kind congregate in a small area to hawk exactly the same goods or services in direct, but apparently quite harmonious, competition with each other. There are areas of al-Qanṭara specialized in clothes, spices, grain and beans, saddle-making, cloth, carpets, raw cotton, paper bags, woodwork, key-cutting, and even weighing scales. Perhaps the most attractive shops in the *sûq* are those of the coppersmiths—the large shops are lined with racks to the ceiling, chock full of gleaming copper vessels of all shapes and sizes, with more on the floor.

The street of the gold and silversmiths (الصاغة • al-Ṣâgha) is behind and slightly separate from the rest of the *sûq*. The easiest way to reach it (unless you get lost in al-Qanṭara and find it by accident) is to return to the Baḥr Yûsuf, turn left (west) along it and turn left again at the next bridge (the fifth west of the waterwheels). Follow this narrow street up a rise, past several crossroads, and down another slope until you reach a twist in the street and see a minaret. Turn sharp left here to find yourself in al-Ṣâgha, a street lined with nothing but gold and silver shops. Glass cases outside each shop display a range of mostly gold and some silver jewelry—chains, pendants, earrings, brooches—but you can have pieces made to order, or have your own jewelry repaired on the spot.

Small markets are held in Fayoum on Tuesdays, some also on Fridays, selling farm produce such as cheese, butter, ghee, eggs, peanuts, dates, beans, and vegetables. Here the country women sit in the sun from 7 or 8 in the morning, having usually walked into town with their heavy baskets on their heads, until mid-afternoon, hopefully displaying their wares to the townfolk, who pick and choose and haggle.

ʻÎn al-Siliyîn

عين السيليين

Take a Sanhûr service taxi, and ask for Siliyîn, which is before Sanhûr, ten to fifteen minutes from Fayoum (1D2). Motorists take the main road north out of Fayoum, passing the Governorate Club on the way out of town. Bear left at the fork at the entrance to Menshât ʻAbdallah, and about 2 kilometers farther on there is a T-junction: turn right here, cross the Ring Road, pass by Zawyat al-Karadsa and through Beni Ṣâleḥ, then, about 5 kilometers from the T-junction, you will reach the entrance to ʻÎn al-Siliyîn on your left, marked by a concrete arch meant to represent a waterwheel.

In the eyes of Fayoumis, the ʻÎn al-Siliyîn gardens, which take their name from one of their two mineral springs, are one of the most important tourist sites in the province—the other being the Birka—and if you have not seen them, you have not seen the Fayoum. They are a favorite pleasure-park for school and university bus trips from Cairo and other parts of Egypt, but they are not likely to excite the foreign visitor.

The park consists basically of a natural hollow with a twisting stream and luxuriant vegetation, but it has been badly spoiled by overcommercialization. A tarmacked road and concrete paths, an ornamental bridge, a children's swimming-pool, a set of chalets, several cafeterias and iced-drinks stands, and tinny, overamplified pop music all conspire to swamp the natural beauty of the place. The springs themselves, whose mineral water is proclaimed to be good for all sorts of things, have all but dried up: ʻÎn al-Shâʻir, now set in an elaborate marble-clad fountain at the far end of the park, was bone dry on my last visit, while ʻÎn al-Siliyîn, down by the stream near the bridge, is now a sad algal trickle under a metal grate. Twenty-five years ago the water used to gush out of both, and was cool and good to drink. Also twenty-five years ago there was a very beautiful, quiet, untouched palm and olive grove, which was a lovely place to wander through or sit in and read a book, but this was completely leveled in the early 1980s for the building of the mineral water bottling plant that has stood idle since a short while after it was opened and is believed by many to have been responsible for the demise of the springs.

'În al-Siliyîn can still be a nice place on a quiet morning; the old watermill at the head of the stream is mildly interesting and a couple of the cafeterias are pleasant enough too, if it is quiet—but on Fridays and public holidays the whole area is drowned in crowds and is best avoided. Al-Siliyîn is situated in the heart of the Fayoum's lush orchard country, so a wander up and down the main road may be more rewarding than a visit to the park itself.

Birkat Qarûn

بركة قارون

Birkat Qarûn (*birkat ·arûn*, often referred to simply as al-Birka), snuggling at 45 meters below sea level into the lowest, northern section of the Fayoum depression, is a large, now salty lake whose history has both dictated and been dictated by the history of the Fayoum. Its salinity, about the same as that of seawater, makes it unfit for both drinking and irrigation, though this has not always been so. Cultivation reaches down to its southern and eastern shores, where fresh water can be brought from the irrigation system, but the entire northern shore is bare desert, uninhabited, and difficult of access.

The Birka and the nearby temple of Qaṣr Qarûn (see page 79) are said by some to take their name from the ruined Greco-Roman city of Karanis to the east, but as the lake was known in the thirteenth century as Birkat al-Ṣêd ('the Fishing Lake') and by this time Karanis had been dead for about eight hundred years, this explanation seems unlikely. Others claim a connection with the word *qarn* ('horn'), and indeed E. W. Lane in the 1820s recorded the name of the lake as Birkat al-Qarn, saying it took its name from the island in the middle, with its horn peak. However, Lane is alone in this: travelers both before and after him give the name of the lake as Qarûn. The popular story is that lake and temple take their name from a character, supposed to have lived around here, who is mentioned in both the Bible and the Quran. In the Bible (Numbers 16), he appears as Korah, who rebels against Moses and is promptly punished by God by being swallowed up in the earth, along with all his family and possessions. In the Quran (al-Qaṣaṣ 76), he appears as a man "exultant in his riches" who finally meets the wrath of God, again by being swallowed up in the earth: “God does not love the exultant.”

An earlier, fuller, and much more revealing version of this story was recorded by the Frenchman Paul Lucas. Riding out from al-Nazla across the desert to visit Qaṣr Qarûn in 1714, he was told the story by his Bedouin companions. A long time ago, “Caron” ruled this area of what is now desert, but which then boasted many towns and more than three thousand villages, with the best climate and the most fertile land in the world. Caron, however, was so evil that he employed magic to bring destruction to his land and turn it into the most sterile and desert place in all Egypt. First, he conjured up a deluge, and then, when the waters had subsided, a great wind that brought so much sand that the whole country was buried forever. This then was the origin of the desert that M. Lucas was now crossing.

Folk memory is long, and this particular ‘fairy tale’ almost certainly has its origins in events of the late Roman period. Ptolemaic and Roman towns did stand here (Theodelphia, Philoteris, Dionysias), and much of the area was cultivated until the decay of the Roman Empire, when local misgovernment and mismanagement led to the loss of good land to the desert and the abandonment of the towns. Even recent reclamation work, which has made the southwestern shore of the Birka green again, has failed to make good the huge losses incurred in late Roman times. Qarûn may thus have been a particularly unpopular Roman governor under whose careless rule this land was deserted, or else a fictional character epitomizing the Roman administration in general. The Biblical and Quranic connotations were probably grafted on later when the similarity between the two stories was noticed.

Coming from Cairo, a right turn 2 kilometers after the Kôm Ôshîm Museum leads to the Birka and on to Wâdi al-Rayyân. From Fayoum, take the Siliyîn road north out of town and pass straight through Beni Ṣâleḥ, al-Siliyîn, and Fidimîn. The road here is lined with orchards enclosed by mud walls and crowded with fruit trees of all sorts as well as vines and the giant yellow-flowering cacti that produce the prickly pear in summer. Between Fidimîn and the next village, Sanhûr, parts of the walls are covered in tangled briars bearing the beautiful pale pink 'baladi' rose in spring. Pass by Sanhûr and reach the Birka about 24 kilometers out of Fayoum.

Those without private transport can take a service taxi to Sanhûr from Fayoum, then another to the Birka. The taxi-boys usually call the Birka 'al-birka,' but to a foreigner might say 'karûn' or 'al-Oburj' (the Auberge). The taxis from Sanhûr to the Birka sometimes go directly north to the Auberge along the asphalt road, but often take the alternative route west then north to Shakshûk, a fishing village on the Birka, and then follow the lake shore east to the Auberge before turning south again to complete a circle back to Sanhûr. To return to Fayoum, you will have to flag down a passing taxi on the lake shore.

The Auberge du Lac (الأوبرج • *al-oburj*), now operated by the Helnan chain, was once a residence of King Farouk and the scene of talks of several world leaders, including Winston Churchill and King Ibn Sa'ûd in February 1945 (1D1; see page 39). There is a promenade along the lake shore east of the Auberge, and westward are several walled-off beaches that cater to the masses in the summer but are bleakly deserted in winter. The usual summer scene at this end of the Birka is one of a calm blue expanse of water, dotted perhaps with a fleet of black fishing craft, bordered by distant bright yellow desert hills. The winter scene can be rather different—the prevailing color usually gray, the water choppy, often wild, the far shore more often than not obscured by the gray gloom that pervades all, and the cold wind biting into your bones. It is not always like this, of course—the blue-and-yellow days can be had in winter too.

It is best if possible to avoid the Auberge area on Fridays and public holidays, when busload upon busload of school and university students from other parts of Egypt come on day-trips, thumping drums and making merry. The Birka on other days is a beautiful, peaceful place. On holidays it can be unbearable. At most times, and in almost all weathers, colorful boats can be commissioned from around the Auberge for a negotiable price per hour.

A few kilometers west of the Auberge, just over the rise known as Gebel al-Zîna, is the well-sited Cafeteria Gebel al-Zîna (1D1; كافتريا جبل الزينة). The food is very good: particularly recommended is the sole *(samak mûsa)*, as good as any you will find in Alexandria. This is a pleasant place to sit and enjoy the view, though I can no longer (as I did in earlier editions of this book) encourage swimming here, or indeed anywhere else in the Birka—the water is not as clean as it used to be.

Farther west again, just east of Shakshûk, are the Oasis Motel (1D2; tel: 084 683-0666), with chalets on the lake shore, and the Panorama Hotel (1D2; tel & fax: 084 683-0757 or 683-0746 or 683-0314), which is clean and smart, with spacious, attractive rooms, and beautifully situated on a small, picturesque bay. There is a restaurant here, and a pleasant terrace café on the bay.

From the Panorama Hotel a road now goes all the way to the western end of the lake and beyond. West of the small fishing village of Shakshûk there are no crowds, and the scenery just gets better as the desert hills on the north shore come closer and become more rugged. The turnoff to Wâdi al-Rayyân is 28 kilometers from the Panorama Hotel. Just before it, on a rise on the left, just after the ugly private resort of al-Rubû‘ on the right, is the village of Tûnis, the St. Ives of Egypt (1B2). Twenty-five years ago, before the road came this way, Tûnis was a remote farming settlement like many others in the Fayoum. Now it is home to a growing colony of potters, writers, artists, and intellectuals from Cairo and elsewhere who have built tasteful (and occasionally not so tasteful) houses here using vernacular (and occasionally not so vernacular) architecture and materials. The Zad al-Mosafer Guest House (tel: 084 682-0180; guesthouse@zadalmosafer.com), run by writer Abduh Gubeir, offers ecolodge-style accommodation; stay here and enjoy the country air, the tranquility, and some of the best views anywhere of the Birka. Three well-known and talented potters, Egyptian Aḥmad Abu Zêd and Swiss husband and wife Evelyne Porret and Michel Pastore, were among the first to make their homes and their studios in Tûnis, and

Evelyne and Michel have also set up a pottery school in the village for local children to learn the craft. Telephone to make an appointment to view the products of Aḥmad's studio (084 682-0357) or of the school (084 682-0405). The entrance to the village is from the small road parallel to the lakeshore road, left off the Wâdi al-Rayyân road, 1 kilometer from the lake.

History of the Birka

Birkat Qarûn today, 45 meters below sea level, has a surface area of 214 square kilometers. It has a maximum depth of just over 8 meters (west of Golden Horn Island) and a volume of 800 million cubic meters; it is 42 kilometers long, and 9 kilometers wide at its broadest point. About 370 million cubic meters of drainage water reach the Birka annually, and as the lake level now stays fairly constant and there are no known outlets, this figure is also taken as the annual rate of evaporation. This means that if the water supply to the Birka were cut off, it would dry up in little over two years. The high rate of evaporation has naturally led to a concentration of salts, and the Birka is now about as saline as seawater, with a ratio of around 34.5 parts per thousand, said to be growing at a rate of 0.4 parts per year. For comparison, sea water ranges between 34 and 37 parts per thousand, while Jordan's Dead Sea has between 300 and 330 parts. The water is less salty in the east and south of the Birka, where the two main drains bring in fresh water.

Large as the Birka now seems, it is but a puddle of its former glory (the Arabic word *birka* means 'pond' or 'pool'). It was certainly much bigger in the past than it is now, but just how big and at what stage in its history are debated points. The evidence on which the various theories are based is sometimes archaeological, sometimes historical, sometimes hydrological, sometimes geological. The Fayoumis' own theory is that the great lake and surrounding swamps were drained by the patriarch Joseph: the Fayoum became the Land of Joseph and the river from the Nile, Joseph's Water—Baḥr Yûsuf. John Ball, in his *Contributions to the Geography of Egypt* published in 1938, worked out a detailed history, which has been only minimally contradicted by the most recent studies. What follows is based on Ball's account.

The Fayoum basin was first excavated by wind action in the early Pleistocene period, and headward erosion of a side-gulley of the Nile led to the breaking in of Nile floodwater through what is now the Lahûn Gap 70,000 years ago in the early Palaeolithic. The depression filled up to form a lake at about 40 meters above present sea level. This lake was in 'free communication' with the Nile—that is, Nile water flowed into the lake during the flood season, and flowed out again to the Nile during the low season. A number of level changes occurred, linked to climatic variations, changes in the level of the Nile, or shifts (eastward or westward) of the course of the Nile. Fluctuations in Neolithic times led to the success or demise of various early agricultural or fishing communities on the lake shore.

Birkat Qarûn

A general recession set in around the beginning of Dynastic times, so that during the Old Kingdom the lake may have been as low as 2 meters below sea level and no longer in free communication with the Nile. Much of the low-lying land was swamp and marsh, good hunting-ground for sporting pharaohs.

In the Twelfth Dynasty (2000–1790 BCE), Amenemhat I, identified with the king known to the Greeks as Lamarres or Moeris, reflooded the lake, bringing its level very rapidly up to 18 meters above sea level. He did this by widening and deepening the existing channel connecting the Fayoum to the Nile (the channel which has become the present-day Baḥr Yûsuf), and by constructing a 5-kilometer embankment from the northern side of the Lahûn Gap at al-Lahûn to the high land of Gebel Abu Ṣîr in the Nile Valley, ensuring that no water, once it reached the entrance to the Fayoum, could escape to the north. Remains of this embankment can still be seen at al-Lahûn (see page 93). Once the channel had been dug, the lake probably took four or five years to fill up.

An initial object in clearing the channel may have been to drain the low-lying marshes along the western desert edge of the Nile Valley, but the net result, and probably the main purpose of the

The History of Birkat Qarûn

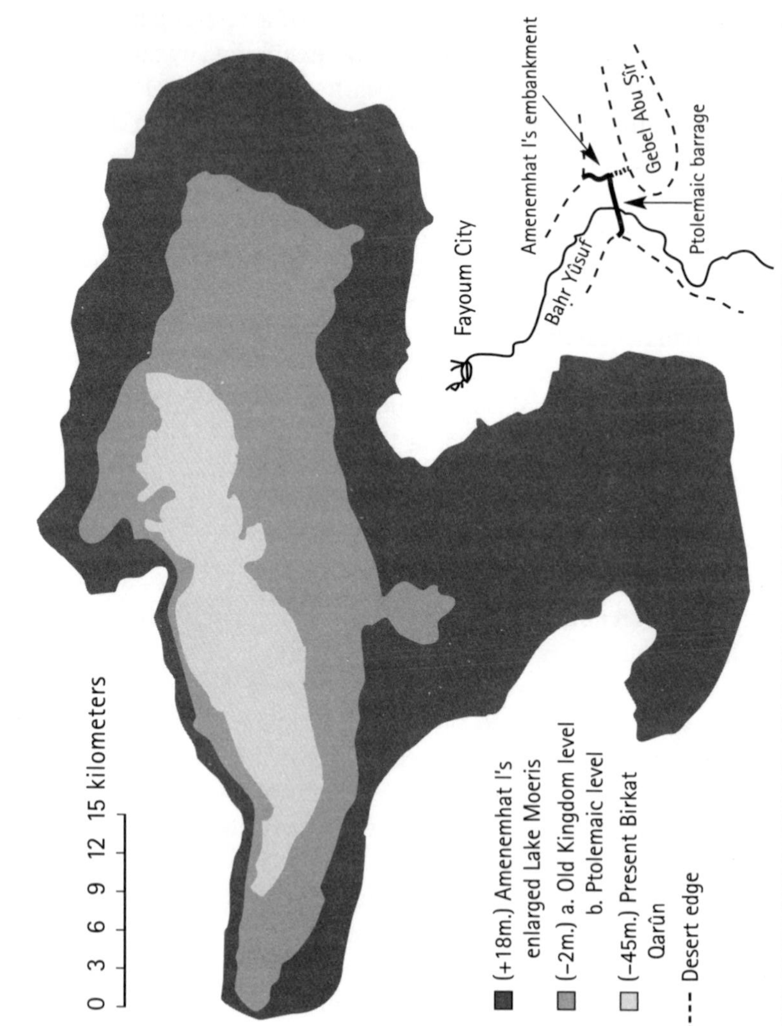

mammoth scheme, was to create an overspill for Nile floodwater (thus protecting Lower Egypt from the disaster of excessively high floods), which could then, in the season of the low Nile, act as a reservoir and return water to the Nile Valley. What Amenemhat I in effect did, then, was to reestablish the free communication between the Fayoum lake and the Nile.

Birkat Qarûn

All Twelfth Dynasty remains in the Fayoum stand at 18 or more meters above sea level—the pedestals of Biahmu (al-Ṣanam), Madînat Mâḍi, Qaṣr al-Ṣâgha, Hawwâra and Lahûn pyramids. The lake level fluctuated seasonally, so that the colossi of Biahmu, at exactly 18 meters, would stand sometimes dry, sometimes surrounded by water. The high land in the southeast, around the capital Shedet (Kimân Fâris), remained untouched by the floodwater throughout the year, but was easily irrigated by side-channels from the main canal with no lifting-gear required, so this land was well cultivated.

The lake, known by the Greeks as Lake Moeris, from the Egyptian words *mer wer*, 'great lake,' still stood at around the same level, possibly a little higher, when Herodotus saw it in the mid-fifth century BCE, and remained there until early Ptolemaic times. The large-scale reclamation of the Fayoum accredited to Ptolemy II was actually begun under Ptolemy I. Amenemhat's barrage from al-Lahûn to Gebel Abu Ṣîr had its southern section dismantled and a new barrage, Gisr al-Bahlawân, was built roughly from west to east, across the mouth of the Lahûn Gap to join up to the middle of the older barrage at al-Lahûn. With sluices in the new barrage across the Baḥr Yûsuf, the flow of water into the Fayoum was now strictly controlled, and only water sufficient for irrigation was allowed in, the excess being diverted northward. It probably took about thirty years to lower the level of the lake to 2 meters below sea level (the level it had been in the Old Kingdom), where it stayed constant for most of the Ptolemaic period, that is from around 300 BCE until just before the beginning of the Christian era. The reclamation under the Ptolemies of about 1,200 square kilometers of good, fertile land led to an agricultural boom, with a large settlement program and the founding of many new towns and villages. Land south of the lake was basin-irrigated from canals branching off the Baḥr Yûsuf, while some land north of the lake was irrigated directly from the lake itself with the use of machinery.

During the Roman decline of the third to fifth centuries, many canals, including the Baḥr Yûsuf, became badly silted up. Consequently much land was lost to the desert and the reduction of inflow caused a further fall in the level of the lake, bringing it down to 36 meters below sea level by the end of the Roman period.

The salinity of the water began to increase. In al-Nabulsi's time (thirteenth century CE), cultivation on the northern shore of the Birka had all but ceased—irrigation with lake water was almost at an end, with one lonely waterwheel in operation. Lucas in 1714 said the lake was bitter in the west, sweet in the east. Pococke, visiting the western end of the lake in the low Nile season in the 1740s reported the water to be almost as salty as the sea. In January 1801, Dr. Martin's horses drank from the eastern end of the lake, though a day later his camels were floundering on a salt-crust at the western end. The lake at that time probably stood at around 40 meters below sea level. When E. W. Lane spent a few days on and around the lake in the summer of 1827, he drank the "brackish" water when his goatskin of fresh water ran out. The salt in it only made him thirstier and he drank more, and more, then resorted to unripe cucumbers. The result of this unwise consumption was five months of dysentery, ophthalmia, and dysentery again.

Underground drainage from the Birka, which acted to slow down the increase in salinity, probably stopped around 1890 when the water level came into equilibrium with the great water-sheet under the Libyan desert at 40 meters below sea level. Hence salinity has increased more rapidly since that time, to the degree that nearly all original species of freshwater fish have now died out, and marine species have been successfully introduced. The level of the Birka has for most of the last hundred years been carefully maintained at 45 meters below sea level.

The lake, its shoreline, and the desert hills to its north are all part of a protected area. The north shore in particular, now more accessible since the construction of a tarmac road at the western end, is a delicate and vulnerable environment. It is worth exploring for the flocks of shy flamingoes and less shy spoonbills that enjoy the quiet shallows in winter, for the extraordinary geological formations of the desert scarp, and for the dramatic views of the lake from the hills.

But this is also an area rich in fossils and prehistoric human sites of great importance, too many of which have already been destroyed by thoughtless four-wheel-drivers. Here is my personal plea: Leave your car on the tarmac and *walk* into the desert. You'll enjoy it so much more on foot anyway, when every step can bring a new discovery, a new vista, a new lungful of fresh air, a new sense of total peace in a still and pristine landscape.

The north shore road leaves the main south shore road at a right turn 8 kilometers west of the Wâdi al-Rayyân junction, opposite a school, and runs for 22 kilometers until it stops abruptly at a dead end in the middle of the desert. You can park your car at any point along this road and walk to an adventure, up hill or down dale. Do beware, though, that much of the ground near the water's edge conceals soft, deep, black mud that doesn't like to let go.

Wâdi al-Rayyân
وادى الريان

Wâdi al-Rayyân ■ وادى الريان

A great new hydrological project, in the best traditions of Amenemhat I and Ptolemy I, was completed in the last quarter of the twentieth century in Wâdi al-Rayyân, a large depression in the desert west of the Fayoum. Water now flows into this originally dry basin, 43 meters below sea level, to form two large lakes (see page 8 for the planning and aims behind this new Moeris). The northern lake lies higher than the southern, so the reed-clad channel linking the two lakes ends in a row of falls a couple of meters high. These are the famous *shallalât*—no Iguazú, perhaps, but they are the only waterfalls in Egypt. Hurry, though, because they are shrinking: the level of the lower lake will continue to rise until the expanding surface area allows a rate of evaporation equal to the amount of water flowing into the lake. The northern lake, because it has an outlet into the southern lake, is only slightly brackish, but the water of the southern lake, with no outlet but evaporation, has already reached a level of salinity approaching that of Birkat Qarûn.

There is no public transportation to Wâdi al-Rayyân. By car, take the road along the southern shore of Birkat Qarûn to its western end. Here, 28 kilometers west of the Panorama Hotel, is the turnoff left for Wâdi al-Rayyân, well marked by a large overhead sign. The road, despite an occasional twist and dogleg, heads south, and in 8.5 kilometers you reach the entrance gate to the Wâdi al-Rayyân Protected Area. The gate is not always staffed, but if it is, you must buy a ticket here for your vehicle and each occupant. Now suddenly you are in clean and wide open desert, which becomes more beautiful, with sculpted yellow dunes, the farther south you travel. Fourteen kilometers from the entrance gate a desert track to the left leads down to the waterfalls and a couple of cafeterias (1A3). This is the area of Wâdi al-Rayyân that is immensely popular, and it can often—especially on Fridays and holidays—be crowded and noisy, almost certainly not what you were expecting. The location for too many videoclips and romantic cinematic scenes, most notably in Youssef Chahine's *al-Muhâgir*, the waterfalls are interesting enough, indeed very pretty if there is nobody around, but unless it is totally deserted you probably won't feel like lingering here.

Continuing south from the waterfalls turnoff, with ever better views of the blue southern lake and yellow dunes (which sometimes encroach on the road, so be careful), 7 kilometers later you come on the left to the dramatic double-crowned butte of Gebel al-Nuhûd (Breast Mountain; 1A4). A path leads down from here then up to the saddle between the crowns. (Some selfish people have already spoiled this special place by driving their cars across the fragile desert surface, and even up onto the saddle itself; please don't make it worse: leave your vehicle on the road and walk.) The views from the hill are spectacular: the indigo lake to the east fringed by reeds, the desert scarp beyond it, and the vast emptiness of desert sweeping south. There is usually nobody here, and this is a fine spot to forget time and drink deep drafts of unspoiled beauty.

Continuing south along the road, 12.5 kilometers beyond Gebel al-Nuhûd there is a ranger post on the right. You can leave your car here and take an interesting walk around the mountain, across dunes and rock pavements, to the springs area and the monastery (see page 68), but the walk is about 10 kilometers each way, so think twice before undertaking it in hot weather. Another 11 kilometers down the road is a signpost left to a "Bird Watching Site" among the reeds on the lake shore, and 4 kilometers farther on are a set of textbook longitudinal dunes up to 30 meters high, with rising peak after peak strung out along a knifeblade edge that runs for several kilometers—their alternative name of seif dunes is taken from the Arabic word for 'sword.' They parallel the shore of an inlet that is the southernmost reach of the southern lake, bordered by reeds and tamarisks, and bursting with birdsong. The road continues east from here, and another 44 kilometers of generally uninteresting, flat desert with occasional views north of the southern Fayoum basin bring you to the Cairo–Asyûṭ desert highway, south of the Lahûn Gap, 92.5 kilometers from the Wâdi al-Rayyân entrance gate.

Wâdi al-Ḥitân ■ وادى الحيتان

The first fossil whale skeletons were discovered in what is now known as Wâdi al-Ḥitân (the Valley of the Whales) in 1902, but it was only recently, as the site's unique and immense importance became more widely recognized, that it was declared a UNESCO World Heritage Site in 2005. The paleontologists are still working, but so far within this small area more than four hundred skeletons of two extinct species of whale have been discovered, along with the fossil remains of other marine life such as sea cows, sea urchins, turtles, crabs, rays, shipworms, and mangroves.

Between 250 and 35 million years ago, much of northern Egypt (as well as other parts of the world as far east as Pakistan) was under the waters of a super-Mediterranean, the Tethys Sea. Around 40 million years ago, the coastline of this great ocean ran more or less through the Fayoum, and Wâdi al-Ḥitân was an area of shallow bays and mangrove swamps that teemed with food for two early predatory whale species, *Basilosaurus isis* and *Dorudon atrox* (the larger Basilosaurus also preyed on the smaller Dorudon). The remains of these whales and other animals and plants became fossilized and buried under layers of rock over millions of years, and after millions more years of erosion the fossils are being exposed again.

What makes the Wâdi al-Ḥitân whales (and similar fossils found in Pakistan) special is the presence of functional hind limbs, which are not present in any modern whale species and are a clear indicator of the evolution of whales from ancient land mammals. These back legs were small, certainly not long enough or strong enough for walking on land (so it is clear that Basilosaurus and Dorudon were entirely aquatic by this time), but they may still have been used to get a grip while coupling.

Tickets for Wâdi al-Rayyân cover your entrance to Wâdi al-Ḥitân, but you can also buy them here if no one was on the gate when you entered Wâdi al-Rayyân. A short way beyond Gebel al-Nuhûd, the right turn to Wâdi al-Ḥitân is signposted. From here it is a bumpy, dusty ride west along a graded desert track of 34 kilometers (perfectly manageable in an ordinary two-wheel-drive vehicle) to the car park and reception area of the site. Here there are toilets, a cafeteria, and a shop selling souvenirs and a very useful 20-page guidebook to the history and fossils of the valley, available in both English and Arabic. You can also buy an interesting DVD documentary about Wâdi al-Ḥitân, in English and Arabic on the one disc.

The guidebook advises you to allow at least two hours for the full 3 kilometer walk, but there is a shorter loop if you don't have the time or energy for the complete tour. Sites along the walk are numbered 1–13, and the guidebook will tell you what you are seeing at each point. There are also well designed information boards and environmentally friendly shaded rest areas at intervals along the route. Apart from the fossils, Wâdi al-Ḥitân is also a place of great natural beauty. Eons of erosion have sculpted the rocks into fantastic shapes, and inscribed them too with the timeless and unknowable script of the gods.

Monasteries in the Fayoum

Monasteries were established early in the Fayoum, particularly between the fourth and sixth centuries, that is, shortly after the birth of monasticism in Egypt's Eastern Desert, and at one stage numbered thirty-five in and around the province. According to tradition, St. Antony, one of the first Desert Fathers and acknowledged founder of Christian monasticism, visited the Fayoum early in the fourth century and inspired many followers here to enter the desert as hermit monks.

Dêr Wâdi al-Rayyân (دير وادى الريان • Wâdi al-Rayyân Monastery) is a loose community of monks who live individually in caves on the west side of Gebel Minqâr, east of the springs area, a 10-kilometer walk from the ranger post on the main road through Wâdi al-Rayyân (see page 65). Each monk's cave is closed to the outside world with masonry and a door and is supplied with electricity by a solar panel. The caves all consist of two rooms: one for living and one for prayer and contemplation. The monks also spend time, if they wish, wandering in the desert, praying and seeking God, but they generally come together in the cave church once a week for communal prayers. Below the monastery, on the valley floor, is the garden, watered by one of the four springs, in which the monks cultivate fresh vegetables; other supplies are brought in by weekly truck.

Dêr al-'Azab (دير العزب • 'Bachelor Monastery') is an important site for Fayoumi Christians (1D3), partly because it contains the more easily accessible of the two principal Christian cemeteries (the other is at Dêr al-Malâk), and partly because it is the burial place of the favorite modern saint, Anba Abrâm, Bishop of the Fayoum and Gîza from 1882 to 1914 (see page 50). The large portrait of Anba Abrâm in one of the chapels in the new church is said, on certain occasions, to reach out and shake hands with a particularly blessed visitor. Carloads and busloads of worshipers, mourners, and pilgrims flood into the monastery on Fridays, Sundays, and Feast Days, but despite the great pull for local Christians, Dêr al-'Azab is likely to hold little if any interest for the foreign visitor. Although the monastery was founded in the twelfth or thirteenth century, very little of the original building remains, and everything now standing appears modern. To reach the monastery from Fayoum, take the Beni Swêf road south out of al-Ḥawâtim. At a fork about 5 kilometers out of town, veer left, and Dêr al-'Azab is on the right after barely 1 kilometer. A service taxi to either Beni Swêf or al-Lahûn from al-Ḥawâtim will drop you at the door of the monastery.

Dêr al-Malâk (دير الملاك • 'Angel Monastery') is a much more interesting, not to say picturesque, monastery than Dêr al-'Azab, and is well worth a visit, in spite of its remoteness (1E3). Proceed as for Dêr al-'Azab, but at the fork bear right, on the road to Qalamshâh *('alamshâh)*. One kilometer from the fork, the road crosses a pretty stream in a small valley; 5 kilometers beyond this, after the second small village (which is actually two villages, Qalhâna *['alhâna]* on the left, Menshât Rabî' on the right, separated by the road), turn left by a storeyard to follow the bank of a canal. After 1 kilometer, you reach a small settlement, where you cross the bridge and continue for 4 kilometers through the desert until you reach the main gate. Don't be put off by the ugliness of this modern entrance: the monastery inside is a real gem. A service taxi for Qalamshâh from al-Ḥawâtim will take you as far as the storeyard at the turnoff, from where the monastery is a rather long but pleasant walk—pleasant, of course, in cool weather only.

Beautifully set on a desert hillside overlooking low, green land, the Monastery of the Archangel Gabriel (sometimes also known as Dêr al-Naqlûn, from the name of the hill) was probably founded in the second half of the fifth century. The church, dedicated to the Archangel Gabriel, dates from the tenth or eleventh century but incorporates elements—most noticeably columns—from earlier structures. Take your shoes off and leave them outside in the yard before entering the church building through a low door. You first step into a vestibule, then into a narrow corridor, before entering the church itself through another small door. In the corridor are the first of the wall paintings for which this monastery is now justly renowned: the others are in the left side aisle and the apse of the church itself. Dated with certainty to the middle of the eleventh century, these treasures were somehow covered over with plaster and memory of them was lost for centuries until they were rediscovered during restoration work in 1991. The paintings—of virgin and child, of apostles and saints, with inscriptions in Coptic—are superb examples of medieval Coptic art, executed with great skill and sensitivity: just look at the assured composition of the standing figures, at the strength and grace of the horses of the equestrian saints, or at the arced strokes of green behind Christ on the cross. These are stunning works of art on any level.

In a side room off the main church lie the remains of the Naqlûn Martyrs. Encased now in embroidered red velvet and under glass, these are the naturally mummified bodies of murdered monks and others that were also found during the restoration work of 1991. Nobody knows who these monks, women, and children were, when they lived and died, or who killed them, but the marks are there: fetters, signs of torture, a missing head, bloodstained clothes, evidence of strangulation. Luckily, the bodies are not open to view, but the gruesome pictures can be had in the monastery shop.

At the back of the monastery are the remains of earlier structures, and in the hills behind the monastery are several caves that were once used as hermitages by monks. Good fun can be had scrambling around the valleys and ridges of the hills, and from the crest there are good views west of the southern part of the Fayoum basin, and east of the Nile valley. To the north is the narrow strip of the Lahûn Gap, and the pyramids of Hawwâra and al-Lahûn may be visible to the north and northeast respectively.

The monastery is usually very quiet, but bus outings do occasionally turn up, particularly on Fridays and holidays. Large crowds congregate on special feast days, and whole families move into the rooms built around the monastery for the last few days of major fasts.

Ancient Sites of the Fayoum

There are sites dating from virtually all eras in the Fayoum, from Neolithic through Dynastic to Ptolemaic and Roman, in various states of preservation. The main sites are presented here in approximately anticlockwise order, starting at Kôm Ôshîm on the Cairo road. They are:

Kôm Ôshîm: Ptolemaic/Roman town; museum. *Entrance fees.*

Dimêh and Qaṣr al-Ṣâgha: Ptolemaic town; Middle Kingdom temple. *Permit required.*

Al-Ṣanam: Middle Kingdom pedestals of two colossi of Amenemhat III.

Qaṣr Qarûn: Well-preserved Ptolemaic temple. *Entrance fee.*

Madînat Mâḍi: Twelfth Dynasty and Ptolemaic temples; ruined town.

Umm al-Burigât: New Kingdom temple and town.

Hawwâra: Middle Kingdom pyramid of Amenemhat III; site of the Labyrinth. *Entrance fee.*

Al-Lahûn: Middle Kingdom pyramid of Senwosret II; embankment of Amenemhat I. *Entrance fee.*

Maydûm: Old Kingdom pyramid of Sneferu. *Entrance fee.*

Umm al-Atl: Ptolemaic/Roman village.

Sêla: Mysterious Old Kingdom pyramid of Sneferu.

Kôm Ôshîm ▪ كوم أوشيم

Entrance fees. The ruins of Karanis at Kôm Ôshîm are among the best preserved, and certainly the most easily accessible, of Ptolemaic/ Roman town sites in the Fayoum (1E1). They lie 25 kilometers from Fayoum city, 56 kilometers from the traffic circle at the Meridien

Pyramids, on the east side of the main Cairo–Fayoum highway, perched on the very rim of the desert, commanding a fine panorama of the rich green lands of the Fayoum basin, with a glimpse of Birkat Qarûn to the west. Coming by any bus from either direction, ask the conductor to put you off at Mat-ḥaf Kôm Ôshîm (متحف كوم أوشيم). In a private car, simply pull into the museum forecourt under the trees.

The *Kôm Ôshîm Museum*, closed for renovations as this edition goes to press, is small but interesting and well laid out, well worth the small entrance fee. It houses artifacts from all over the Fayoum (and a few from other parts of the country), but many of the province's treasures were taken to the Egyptian Museum in Cairo and the Greco-Roman Museum in Alexandria before the Kôm Ôshîm Museum was built in 1974. Thus at the moment the museum unfortunately has only one of the famous Fayoum Portraits (see page 91) and no crocodile mummies.

Facing the entrance is a colossal limestone head of a Roman god from Karanis, thought to be either Neptune or Serapis. To the left are a number of fascinating Roman terracotta figures from Kimân Fâris, including a suitably debauched-looking Bacchus and a beautifully grotesque monkey figure. Also from Kimân Fâris are some Roman oil-lamps and an interesting series of small terracotta ladies' heads; notice that the hairstyle on each head is different—these are said to be tonsorial samples for Roman matrons to choose from when visiting their hairdressers. From Hawwâra, there is a lively limestone carving of Venus emerging (perhaps 'squirming' would be a better word), in a not particularly aphrodisiac manner, from her shell. Other Roman exhibits include bronze and gold coins (both Republican and Imperial), glassware, and two large granite feet (not a pair). The small Coptic mummy of a fifteen-year-old boy with its portrait panel still in place, dating from the fourth or fifth century CE, was found at Dêr al-Banât, in the southeast of the Fayoum near Dêr al-Malâk, in 1982. Among the pharaonic exhibits are two perfectly preserved and superbly painted mummy cases, complete with mummies, one belonging to a woman called Mahia from the Twelfth Dynasty, the other to a priest of the Twenty-sixth Dynasty called Bak-hotep; ushabtis; Middle Kingdom alabaster canopic jars from Hawwâra; necklaces; and perfume jars. The four delightful wooden models—a country house with its inhabitants, and three boats—were found recently at Hawwâra. One of the most interesting little pieces is a small, simple pot in the form of a basket of exactly the kind still used by Egyptian laborers today for carrying earth and shifting rubble, known as a *ma·ṭaf,* and manufactured in great numbers in the village of al-'Agamiyîn on the road to Ibshawây. Upstairs are Coptic textiles and icons, medieval carved wooden panels, and—inexplicably—parts of Muḥammad 'Ali Pasha's dinner service and silverware.

Immediately behind the museum are the extensive ruins of *Karanis* (separate entrance fee), a town founded by the Ptolemaic Greek settlers in the third century BCE and continuing as a Roman town, probably until the early fifth century CE. Karanis was primarily a frontier settlement, serving as a point of departure for caravan traffic and as a station for the desert police. Yet the surrounding land was also cultivated, and was probably irrigated, at least in part, directly from the lake, whose waters had by this time attained a degree of salinity too high for human consumption but still low enough for use on the land. Drinking water was taken from the canal system.

The town, which is thought to have had a population of around three thousand, was built mostly of unburnt mud brick at about sea-level on or near the shore of the then much larger Lake Moeris. The walls of many of the buildings still stand, often plastered on the interior, and streets and lanes can be made out. Lying around the houses are the remains of millstones and granite olive presses, giving an inkling of the daily life of some of the inhabitants.

In the center of the town, standing proud on a massive foundation of rough-hewn stones, is the main temple, built of finished limestone blocks. Above the entrance (eastern end) is an inscription in Greek, a dedication to the Roman emperor Nero, but although the temple has survived well, there are no other inscriptions. It was dedicated to a form of Sobek. From the roof there is a good view of the ruined town all around, the Fayoum basin to the south, and the second, smaller, temple on a rise to the north. The plan of the two temples is similar, but the northern temple has no inscriptions at all.

The long, low, sandy-colored building between the museum and the ruins was once the villa of Sir Miles Lampson, British high commissioner (later, as Lord Killearn, British ambassador) in Egypt, first-rate practitioner of British gunboat diplomacy on dry land. It was Killearn who on February 4, 1942, at a critical stage in the war in North Africa and a time of strong anti-British feeling in Egypt, surrounded King Farouk's 'Abdîn Palace in Cairo with British tanks. He then 'requested' the king, whose tenure of the throne depended very much on British good will, to ask Naḥâs Pasha, a personal enemy of the king but thought to be pro-British, to form a non-coalition government. The king complied. His alternative was abdication and exile, a fate that caught up with him ten years later. Killearn left Egypt quietly in 1946 and was replaced by a more diplomatic diplomat, Sir Ronald Campbell.

Dimêh al-Sibâ' ▪ ديميه السباع and Qaṣr al-Ṣâgha ▪ قصر الصاغة

An excursion to these two sites on the northern side of Birkat Qarûn is one of the most interesting in the Fayoum, rewarding and memorable as much for the desert and lake scenery as for the historical interest of the sites themselves (1C1). Even those without the slightest interest in antiquities will enjoy this trip and cannot fail to be impressed by the magnificent, lonely ruins of Dimêh. However, the visit is not to be undertaken lightly. The sites are extremely remote and a long way from help should you run into trouble. If approaching by car—four-wheel drive only—from Kôm Ôshîm, be sure that your tank is full, that you have plenty of water (for your radiator and for yourselves), and food—it could be a long day. Also carry two boards, which you may need in soft sand, and do not drive alone—have at least three people in your party, preferably more. Qaṣr al-Ṣâgha is about 30 kilometers from Kôm Ôshîm, Dimêh a further 9 kilometers, and you should allow at least an hour and a half for the whole 40 kilometers. Note that since 1992, visits to Dimêh and Qaṣr al-Ṣâgha have been allowed only with a permit from the Supreme Council for Antiquities headquarters in 'Abbasiya in Cairo.

Take the signposted road that runs west off the main Cairo–Fayoum road through the industrial estate just opposite the Kôm Ôshîm Museum. This soon becomes a desert track, which you must follow carefully–it is clearer in some parts than others. If you lose the track, as we once did, you will be in trouble. We ended up too far south in a large basin of soft sand and extricated our four-wheel-drive truck only by ripping pieces off it to put time after time under the wheels, while a packet of potato chips and a tray of sticky, home-made *basbûsa* helped maintain moral and physical strength. You will find yourself heading roughly northwest, then west. There are cairns and other markers in places where the track becomes temporarily indistinct.

The towering ruins of Dimêh al-Sibâ' (Dimêh 'of the Lions') are visible on the western horizon from a long way off, looking more like a North European prehistoric stone circle than the ruins of a Middle Egyptian Ptolemaic city, but the small temple of Qaṣr al-Ṣâgha ('Goldsmiths' Palace') is well camouflaged halfway up the escarpment to the north and is not easily spotted from a distance.

Qaṣr al-Ṣâgha is a slightly puzzling temple now believed to date from the Middle Kingdom, although more precise dating is impossible due to the lack of inscriptions, friezes, or statues. The building is small, consisting only of a corridor with seven large recesses and a few side apartments. Its fascination lies in the peculiarity of its construction. Instead of the usual regular courses of uniform blocks that one sees in other ancient buildings, the whole temple, including the façade, is a remarkable jigsaw of blocks of all shapes and sizes, neatly fitted together by the careful cutting of strange angles, notches, and corners. It looks almost Aztec, and might seem more in place on an Andean mountaintop. A mysterious narrow passage on the right, ending in a peephole into the main doorway, will exercise your mind as well as your waistline. The view from here of the flat, low plain stretching away to Birkat Qarûn and the Fayoum basin beyond gives a good idea of the original size of the ancient Lake Moeris, which once came right up to the temple.

Nine kilometers southwest of the temple, the ruins of the Ptolemaic city of Dimêh al-Sibâʿ and its temple stand high on what was once a promontory in the lake. Climbing the hill, past parts of a rough outer stone wall, and scrambling over mounds of broken pottery, one comes to the very impressive saw-tooth remains of a huge enclosure wall of white mud brick. Towering up to 10 meters high, and sometimes 5 meters wide, the walls are a magnificent testimony to the durability of the humble mud brick. In the center of this large enclosure is the ruined temple, built of rough stone and immediately surrounded by a mud-brick curtain wall. The temple was dedicated to Soknopaios (a form of Sobek) and Isis.

Although currently not allowed, another way of reaching Dimêh, but not Qaṣr al-Ṣâgha, is to hire a fisherman and his boat from Shakshûk (on the south side of the lake) to ferry you across the lake in an hour or two and wait while you walk the 2 kilometers to the ruins. You must allow at least six hours for this trip. Approaching from the lake, you come first to a well-made and well-preserved 400-meter-long road of large blocks, which leads in triumphal style past rows of ruined houses directly up to the temple enclosure. On the east side of the road, the squat, white, mud-brick remains of a large building are particularly interesting. In the center, a passageway leads down into a perfectly preserved set of cellars. The first chamber has a marvelous mud-brick dome; the others are vaulted, and, with their intact plaster finish, look modern. The cellars are deliciously cool on a hot day.

In antiquity, Dimêh was known as the Island of Soknopaios (although it probably ceased to be an island, due to the falling water level, before the city was founded), and was a secure starting point for trade routes to oases in the Western Desert. Imagine trading caravans sailing slowly across the lake from the south, spending hours unloading on the quay of Dimêh, preparing for the arduous journey ahead, then spending their last night in a town before leaving civilization behind for weeks of desert.

Al-Ṣanam الصنم ■ 'The Idol'—The Pedestals of Biahmu

The remains of two large stone pedestals that once supported colossi of Amenemhat III stand just north of the small village of Biahmu, some 7 kilometers north of Fayoum (1D2). There is not a lot to see at the site, but the setting is quite beautiful and the two large, somewhat ruinous, but essentially complete stone piles, light yellow in color, and now partly supported by Department of Antiquities bricks, are not a little mysterious.

The new Cairo–Fayoum highway now bypasses al-Ka'âbi al-Gadîda about 23 kilometers south of the Kôm Ôshîm Museum, 6 kilometers north of Fayoum. Here a small turnoff to the west leads immediately into the village of Biahmu. The walk from here if you arrive by public transport or choose to leave your car at this point, takes about fifteen minutes. It is possible to take your car through the village, but the road is narrow, and you may have difficulty turning your vehicle around at the end of the village to come back. From the main road, proceed 200 meters into the village and turn right at the fork. After another 400 meters you reach a bridge over a small canal: cross it and turn right (and if you have come this far in your car, leave it here). Follow the canal to the next bridge and turn right to walk along a mud-walled lane through fields and palm groves. From here you will see the pedestals ahead of you. An easier route now (since the old Sinnûris railway line was pulled up and turned into a road) is to turn right on the Ring Road when arriving from Cairo and after 1.7 kilometers turn right again, onto the new Sinnûris road. Just after the village of Biahmu, 4 kilometers from the Ring Road, the pedestals appear in the fields to the right, a short walk from the road.

The walk to al-Ṣanam (from either direction) is very pleasant, and the fresh, soft, sandy color of the two pedestals, standing about 100 meters apart, presents an attractive contrast to the rich green of the very fertile surrounding countryside. How much more striking the scene must have been thirty-eight centuries ago, with the pedestals sheer and neat, each surmounted by a majestic red quartzite seated colossus of Amenemhat III, the immense Lake Moeris stretching from the base of the pedestals to the northern horizon. The pedestals probably stood about the same height as they do now, about 8 meters, and the colossi, according to Petrie's reconstruction, probably towered a further 13 meters. Each colossus and pedestal was surrounded by an enclosure wall of the same solid blocks as the pedestals.

In the thirteenth century CE, Nabulsi saw the two colossi almost intact, one facing west, the other east, but relates that persistent rumors of hidden treasure had led to the removal of their tops. The colossi, however, were solid and yielded nothing but their dignity. Nabulsi also describes a pool near the colossi reputed to cure all ills, and into which, in faith or hope, the local population threw objects and money.

In the seventeenth century, Father Vansleb saw part of one colossus, and by 1801, when Dr. Martin visited Biahmu, the colossi had all but disappeared. In 1888, Professor Petrie removed a number of fragments and passed them on to the Ashmolean Museum in Oxford, which now holds forty-seven pieces. The best preserved is the nose of one colossus, which is on display in the museum's Egyptian Sculpture Gallery. Other fragments were apparently left in situ by Petrie, but these have since disappeared, and now no trace of the colossi remains at al-Ṣanam.

The purpose of the colossi has not been agreed upon. It is unusual in Egypt to find statuary so completely isolated, so they have been explained as markers of a harbor on the ancient Lake Moeris (though no evidence of a harbor has been found); as a special monument to the great achievements of Amenemhat III in the province; or as being somehow related to the main temple of Sobek at Kimân Fâris, 6 kilometers away. Christopher Kirby, who carried out new studies on the site in the 1990s, believes that the enclosure walls represent twin, open-court, solar temples; the highly polished quartzite statue of the pharaoh in the center of each would have shone brilliantly in the sun.

Watch out for little owls roosting on the pedestals. When I took a Fayoumi friend, who had never even heard of al-Ṣanam, to visit the site early one morning in 1982, he was so impressed by his two-minute inspection that he sat down on a rock to read his newspapers,

The ruins of Karanis, Kôm Ôshîm

Al-Ṣanam: pedestal of a seated colossus of Amenemhat III at Biahmu

Mud bricks left to dry in front of the ancient wall of Shidmôh

◁Inside the
Ptolemaic temple
of Qaṣr Qarûn

The Middle Kingdom
pyramid of Senwosret II
at al-Lahûn

The ruins of the Ptolemaic village of Bacchias, Umm al-Atl

Ptolemaic lions guard the temple of Tebtunis, Umm al-Burigât

The Middle Kingdom temple of Qaṣr al-Ṣâgha

▷ The mud-brick enclosure wall at Dimêh al-Sibâ'

The ancient road and walls of Dimêh al-Sibâ'

Sobek, the Fayoum's ancient patron crocodile deity, in a relief at Madînat Mâḍi

Inside the Middle Kingdom temple of Qaṣr al-Ṣâgha

▷The pyramid of Hawwâra, built for the Twelfth Dynasty king Amenemhat III

The mysterious Old Kingdom pyramid of Sêla

The Middle Kingdom temple of Madînat Mâḍi, with a Ptolemaic sphinx

One of the Ptolemaic lions at Madînat Mâḍi

leaving me to explore alone. A little owl, roosting near the top of the western pedestal, watched my movements carefully as I wandered around the base of his perch, viewing and photographing the pile from different angles. His eyes were wide, and his little brown body bobbed up and down, as he seemed to observe me with intense curiosity and rising alarm. The bobbing became more agitated, the eyes grew wider, and his mood apparently changed to sheer indignation as I had the audacity to climb to the top of *his* pedestal. When I came too close he flew off to sit huffily in a nearby palm, and left me to enjoy the early, soft, oblique sunlight on the palms, trees, and fields all around. In 2001, when I visited the site for the first time in nineteen years, the vegetation had grown higher among the fallen blocks, but as I arrived a little owl ducked and hopped from block to block then flew off, yes, to a nearby palm. I'm sure he recognized me.

Qaṣr Qarûn قصر قارون ▪ 'Palace of Qarûn' (pronounced *·aṣr ·arun*)

Entrance fee. This is a well-preserved Ptolemaic temple, about 45 kilometers from Fayoum town, in the northwestern corner of the province (1B2). It is well worth a visit despite the long journey. For the origin of the name, see page 54.

Take a service taxi from Cairo or from Fayoum to Ibshawây (1C2), then a second service taxi from there to the village of Qarûn, alighting after about an hour at the temple, which is very close to the road, just before Qarûn. To get back you will have to wait for a passing taxi and flag it down. On the way back, try to arrive in Ibshawây either well before or well after 2pm, the weekday rush-hour, when finding any kind of transport to Fayoum or Cairo is very difficult.

By private car, coming from Fayoum, take the Ibshawây road west out of town (2B2), passing first through the small town of Sinaru and then along an almost straight road through the fields. Rich orchards (in March and April, pink with apricot blossom) and vineyards under cover of giant prickly-pear cactus plants line the approach to Ibshawây, which is the capital of one of the Fayoum's six 'centers' or administrative districts, and is thus a very busy town. Then, just beyond Ibshawây, the road traverses one of the province's small, twisting valleys, the Maṣraf al-Wâdi ('Valley Drain'), which drains most of the western part of the Fayoum. At this point it is particularly beautiful. The sides are rocky and sandy; the bed is half tamed, half wild—small fields of neat crops are set off by rushes and other wild plants around a busy, twisting, braided stream. This is a uniquely Fayoumi landscape that you will not see anywhere else in Egypt.

Beyond the village of al-Shawâshna the land drops away on the right of the road, and there are fine views (if you're not stuck in the back of a service taxi) of the lake and the surrounding countryside, which in March and April has many striking fields of the bright orange marigold, known in Arabic as *'abbâd al-·amar*, 'worshiper of the moon.' The sunflower in Arabic is *'abbâd al-shams*, 'worshiper of the sun.' Marigolds and the white, daisy-like *shîḥ* (camomile), also extensively grown in this area, are highly profitable crops used in the manufacture of medicines. About 20 kilometers beyond al-Shawâshna, Qaṣr Qarûn appears on the left in the desert, a short walk from the road—you cross sea-level about halfway between the road and the temple.

Coming from Cairo, take the road that follows more or less closely the south shore of the Birka. The views along here—of olive groves, the ever-changing lake, and the barren bluffs of the north shore—become increasingly stunning the farther west you travel. When you reach the turnoff left to Wâdi al-Rayyân, 28 kilometers west of the Panorama Hotel, keep going straight on along the lake shore. After 10 kilometers the road turns south and reaches the village of Qûta (pronounced *·ûta*) in another 3 kilometers. Turn right as you reach the canal running through the village then immediately left over a bridge and left again to gain the other side of the canal and travel east. Qaṣr Qarûn appears on the right after 4 kilometers. When you finish your visit, continue east along this road to reach the Wâdi al-Rayyân road in 6 kilometers; turn left here to get back to the lake road in 1 kilometer.

The temple ('Palace' of Qarûn is a misnomer) is known to be Ptolemaic (323–30 BCE), but has not been dated more precisely due to the absence of inscriptions. Built of blocks of yellow limestone, it is substantially complete, although the exterior has been partially restored by the Antiquities Department, and parts of the internal structure have been reinforced. It appears small from the outside, but inside is a veritable maze of chambers, corridors, cellars, tunnels, stairways, upper rooms of all sizes at different levels, and numerous nooks and crannies, making it a fascinating place to explore—take a torch, or candles. Many rooms are infested with bats; there may also be snakes and scorpions, so mind your step. There are small lizards too that look like baby crocodiles—quite fitting for a temple dedicated to the crocodile god. There are no inscriptions, but over the entrance flies the winged sun, and on the roof (reached by either of two square spiral staircases) is a neat but headless relief of two figures: the crocodile god Sobek on the left, a king on the right. There is a good view from the roof, of the desert to the south and west, the cultivated land to the north and east, and the desert escarpment and (sometimes, depending on the light) the Birka to the north.

Around the temple are the ruins of Dionysias, a Greco-Roman town and garrison, but the mostly mud-brick remains are not as well-preserved as other ancient towns in the Fayoum. The town is thought to date from the third century BCE and was probably abandoned in the fourth century CE. Remains of plant stalks in the sand and even small trees trained up walls suggest that the area in and around the town was once fertile; and indeed, town and temple once stood on the shore of the shrinking lake.

Early European travelers undertook arduous and sometimes dangerous excursions to Qaṣr Qarûn (the round trip by horse from al-Nazla took eighteen hours) under the misapprehension that they were visiting the famous Labyrinth of classical times, as described by Herodotus and Strabo. Pococke in 1743 thought the temple was "without doubt" the remains of that magnificent building, while Paul Lucas in 1714 innocently believed he was the first modern traveler to see the Labyrinth. Lucas, incidentally, gives a good drawing and detailed description of the temple, but his claim to have visited more than 150 rooms is exaggerated. For the real site of the Labyrinth, see page 89.

Madînat Mâḍi مدينة ماضى ▪ 'Mâḍi's City'

These temples (Twelfth Dynasty and Ptolemaic) and ruined town lie in the desert about 30 kilometers southwest of Fayoum (1C3). The trip is not an easy one, but the well-preserved ruins of the temple are very interesting, and make the effort worthwhile. The site can be reached on foot from al-Barins (service taxi to al-Gharaq *[al-ghara·]*, then another to al-Barins) in about 4 kilometers. Another possibility would be to hire a motorbike taxi from al-Minya or Abu Gandîr. We made our first visit to Madînat Mâḍi by bus to al-Minya, then (after being stood up by our supposed guide) perched on the mudguards of an obliging but very slow tractor all the way to the ruins. The driver and his lads waited for us while we looked around the temple; then we in turn waited for them while they took sledgehammer and wedge to the limestone crust of the desert nearby, and loaded their trailer with the broken rock. We returned to al-Minya in the same regal but somewhat insecure fashion as we had come, then proceeded to Fayoum by service taxi—more conventional, but much less fun.

By car, take the Iṭsa road south out of Fayoum, pass directly through Iṭsa (1D3) and come, a short way out of town, to a fork. Take the left fork, which will lead you through Shidmôh (see page 85) to a bridge in the village of Abu al-Nûr, 4.3 kilometers from the fork. Cross the bridge and turn immediately right to follow the edge of the canal westward. After 4.5 kilometers, you will reach a branch canal: turn left to follow this on its south bank, crossing to its north bank after 1 kilometer. Continue to follow the canal for 4.2 kilometers before crossing it again to follow a narrow track alongside a small canal, passing a small village on the left. Head for a cemetery and follow the track southwestward through reclaimed farmland to enter the desert. Aim for a stone building (the dig house) on the rise ahead, but don't leave the marked track, even though at one point it seems to turn in the wrong direction. Just behind the house, over the rise, are the temples of Madînat Mâḍi. It is possible to take your car all the way to the dig house, but you do so at your own risk—the last section on the slope up to the house is quite sandy, but you shouldn't get stuck if you keep your speed up.

The stone temple of Madînat Mâḍi, built by Amenemhat III and Amenemhat IV in the Twelfth Dynasty, and dedicated to Renenutet, the serpent goddess, in conjunction with Sobek, the crocodile god, is attractively set in an elongated hollow. Much of this hollow is usually filled with soft sand, which tends to enhance the romantic, desert atmosphere of this very quiet spot. Every few years, the Department of Antiquities clears the sand away, and with the cleaning operation more of the temple becomes visible, but the sand always comes back. There is an avenue of sphinxes and lions, full of character. One reclining lion, with a fine ruff and beard, looks more like an Elizabethan court chamberlain than anything else. The two unusual female winged creatures are Greek sphinxes. The temple walls, in a pleasant light yellow limestone, bear many reliefs, including some splendid feet along the processional way. Inside the sanctuary there are hieroglyphic inscriptions with cartouches of the two Amenemhats, and pedestals of several statues, only the finely carved feet of which remain. Back to back with the main temple is a Ptolemaic addition, with an altar, some worn Greek inscriptions, and a splendid relief of Sobek, teeth and all.

In the 1990s, the Italian expedition working at Madînat Mâḍi discovered a hitherto unsuspected Ptolemaic temple under the mound of rubble beside the Middle Kingdom temple. It was built of mud brick, with stone portals, its axis at right angles to the older temple. Adjacent to this temple, another building has recently been revealed, with unusual stone capitals on mud-brick pillars and painted plaster decoration on the walls in imitation of marble. As you walk back over the mound to your car, you will see occasional lines of mud brick and palm beams under your feet: these are the walls and roofs of buildings waiting to be unchoked from centuries of debris and sand.

To the southeast of the temple are the ruins of the mud-brick and fired-brick town. The local story is that Abu Zêd al-Hilâli, a popular, semi-fictitious warrior-hero, who led his tribes from the desert of Nejd through Egypt to Tunisia in the eleventh century CE, arrived at the town on his journey and asked the ruler, King Mâḍi, for food and shelter. Mâḍi refused, so Abu Zêd razed the town, killed the king and all his subjects, took all the food he needed, and proceeded on his way. Hence the ruins of 'Mâḍi's City.'

From the rise above the temples, there are good views of the Fayoum basin to the east, the Gharaq basin to the south, and the bare desert to the north and west. There is a quality of desert air that makes these fringe areas of cultivation particularly beautiful, and there is always something dramatic and heroic in the meeting of hard-won green land and noble desert.

For a more scenic route back to Fayoum, when you reach the main canal again and cross the bridge, turn left, then take the first turn right. This road takes you in 3 kilometers to the western end of Abu Gandîr; as you meet the main road leaving the village, turn left, then turn right at the bottom of the hill and follow the canal. This road twists up, down, around, and through several of the Fayoum's distinctive, attractive valleys, terraced and intensively farmed. You will meet three T-junctions on this route: at the first, turn right; at the second, turn left; and at the third, turn right onto the main road from Ibshawây to Fayoum, which you enter at its western end.

Umm al-Burigât أم البريجات ▪ 'Place of the Towerlets'

Umm al-Burigât, the ruined town and temple of Tebtunis, about 30 kilometers from Fayoum city on the southern edge of the province, cannot be reached by public transport (1D4). By car, take the Iṭsa road, which leaves Fayoum in the southwest at Shêkh Ḥasan, west of al-Ḥawâtim. The first village on the right is Abgîg, where the obelisk of Senwosret I, now erected outside Fayoum city on the Cairo road, used to lie broken in a field (see page 41). Pass directly through the dull and rather ugly town of Iṭsa, capital of the southwestern region of the Fayoum, then, shortly out of town at a main fork in the road, bear left.

Now, before and after the small village of Shidmôh • شدموه, first on one side of the road and then on the other, appear the substantial ruins of an old retaining wall made of fired-brick and mortar, and in some parts faced with cut limestone (1D3). The course of the wall is very irregular, as it snakes its way through the fields: this may be due to the old belief that a crooked wall was stronger than a straight one, or perhaps because of complicated land boundaries. When Dr. Martin passed by here in 1801, he was particularly impressed by the solid construction of this "magnificent" wall, which was 8 kilometers long and 6 meters high. It started at Defennu (east of Iṭsa), approached the major village of al-Minya (at that time more important than Iṭsa), and turned south through Shidmôh. Al-Minya's full title is Minyat al-Ḥêt, 'Port of the Wall.' The wall's evident purpose had been to retain water after the flood on its southern and eastern sides for the old system of basin irrigation (see page 6), but some time before Dr. Martin's visit a major, irreparable breach had occurred, sweeping away 60 meters of the wall near Shidmôh and leaving large blocks littered far away on the downstream side. The French doctor's Bedouin companions told him that the Maṣraf al-Wâdi, the deep ravine that runs from al-Minya to al-Nazla, had been formed by the deluge from the breach. Whether this is true or not, it is certainly true that al-Nazla thereafter had an increased water supply, much of which could not be used and flooded low land around the Birka, while large parts of the former basin east of Shidmôh remained uncultivable. The Bedouin of the area had hopes of rebuilding the wall, but this was never achieved and later became unnecessary as perennial irrigation was introduced. The wall was built in the Ptolemaic period, but the brick and masonry facings that can be seen in places are of later Roman date.

Beyond Shidmôh, immediately after the bridge in Abu al-Nûr, the road forks again. Here, you take the left fork, but note the following interesting detour:

The right fork leads to the small market town of al-Gharaq al-Sulṭâni (usually known as al-Gharaq, pronounced *al-ghara·*), in the south-western bulge of the Fayoum basin (1C4). The name of al-Gharaq comes from the root for 'submerge' or 'drown,' and could perhaps be translated as 'The Swamp'; and indeed until recently a sizeable lake occupied much of the area, which was famed in ancient times for its papyrus thickets. Nowadays it is better known for its watermelons, which grow very well in the sandy soil here, and which in season (May–July) pour out of al-Gharaq piled high on little Toyota or Datsun trucks in quite astonishing and mouth-watering quantities.

Mud brick (the traditional building material throughout the Fayoum) is very little used here, the houses in all the villages and in al-Gharaq itself, as in other desert fringe areas, being built of rough-cut blocks of the locally quarried light yellow limestone, often plastered and painted. This gives a much cleaner, perhaps more spartan, appearance to the settlements, and al-Gharaq, particularly on market days (Saturdays and Wednesdays), with scores of saddled donkeys hitched up along the main street, has a distinct frontier atmosphere about it. This is quite appropriate, as, until not so very long ago, the town was a major starting-point for caravans to the Western Desert. Also, right up until the nineteenth century, al-Gharaq had to defend itself against frequent Bedouin raids, and had walls to the purpose.

There are a number of small *birak* ('ponds') in this area, the largest of which, Birkat Abu Ṭâlib, named after a local shêkh whose tomb stands nearby, lies south of the main road west of al-Gharaq, between the villages of Abu Glêl and al-Ḥagar ('The Stone'). It is a popular drive-in tractor-wash and swimming spot, but the prickly weeds that float about just below the surface can be rather alarming. The locals say it is extremely deep, even bottomless, and the children say it is haunted. It also produces very good fish. Just past Birkat Abu Ṭâlib, a right turn leads to the hamlet of 'Ank and a long string of beautiful white sand dunes in a large patch of desert surrounded by fertile land, called Gebel 'Ank. On Shamm al-Nesîm, the ancient Egyptian festival celebrating the end of winter, the locals promenade and picnic on the dunes of Gebel 'Ank and 'smell the breeze' of summer.

The main road leads eventually to a village marked on maps as al-Emir ('The Prince'), but known to the locals as al-Barins, said to be a corruption of 'Prince' and named after an English prince who once lived there. From al-Barins it is possible to walk, in about an hour, to Madînat Mâḍi.

For Umm al-Burigât, take the left fork, which brings you first to the large village of Tuṭûn • تطون, which probably takes its name from the ancient Tebtunis. Just before the end of the village, take a right turn, which takes you in 4 kilometers to Baḥr al-Gharaq, the canal hugging the desert edge.

A short way left along the canal is Qaṣr al-Bâsil, the grand home of a well-known figure in Fayoumi history, Ḥamad Bâsha al-Bâsil, who, himself a Bedouin, led a Bedouin uprising on 12 March 1919 as part of the revolution led by Sa'd Zaghlûl against British rule. The insurgents attacked police posts and lost 400 men.

Turn right to keep the canal on your left for a couple of kilometers until the next bridge, which you cross to reach the desert and the ruins of Umm al-Burigât. The journey takes about an hour from Fayoum.

As elsewhere, the ordinary houses of Umm al-Burigât were built of mud brick, and substantial sections of their walls still stand (many now capped for preservation), some with the original plaster in place, occasionally with colored wall paintings discernable. Meanwhile, the temple was built of quarried stone. This same pattern of priorities can be observed in most Egyptian villages today—private houses are usually built of mud brick, or more recently burnt brick or white brick, while the mosques and churches are built of stone. The visible remains of the town are Ptolemaic/Roman, but the site is thought to have been originally a New Kingdom settlement and continuously inhabited into Islamic times.

The temple is not well preserved, little remaining of the walls, but the long, paved sacred way is more or less intact. It is dedicated, as usual, to the crocodile god Sobek. The two large and rather grand carved lions at the northern end are Greek, and there are many fragments of Greek-style columns of fine white limestone in an area jutting west off the main axis at the southern end. The fragments of wall, the paving, and the sphinxes are of the local, coarser, yellow limestone, and what remains is very similar in general appearance to the much more complete stone temple at Madînat Mâḍi. Very little is to be seen in the way of reliefs. A cache of mummified crocodiles (now removed) was discovered here at the beginning of the twentieth century.

Hawwâra Pyramid هرم هوارة ■ *haram hawwâra*

Entrance fee. Take a Lahûn service taxi and get out at Hawwâra, about 9 kilometers from Fayoum (1E3). Cross the bridge, enter the village, and turn right at a T-junction. Follow this road out of the village and along the north bank of the Baḥr Yûsuf, until a left turn takes you to the pyramid in another 3 kilometers or so.

Motorists can follow the same route (taking the Beni Swêf road out of al-Ḥawâtim), or else take a more scenic route: arriving from Cairo at the Obelisk of Abgîg at the entrance to Fayoum (2E1), turn left. After less than a kilometer turn left at a T-junction, then 1 kilometer farther on, turn right. After encountering the Ring Road, this road then crosses the deep, wide cut of Maṣraf al-Baṭs. Pass through the small village of Demu and enter the desert, which at this point is unfortunately marred by garbage. Turn right at a T-junction and you will see the pyramid ahead.

The pyramid, like that at al-Lahûn, is now a ruinous lump of millions of dark mud bricks (having long ago lost its limestone casing), looking from a distance like a natural plum-pudding hill. Arriving at the pyramid's east side, you pass through the remains of a necropolis, which extends around to the north side. You may have fun exploring this area, but beware of deep, vertical tomb shafts.

The pyramid was built to confuse tomb-robbers, with the entrance on the southern (instead of the usual northern) side and an intricate arrangement of internal passages. You can peek into the entrance and walk a few steps down the sloping passage, but ground water currently stops you from going any farther. When entered in the nineteenth century, the pyramid was found to contain two sarcophagi, one for Amenemhat III and one for his daughter, Nefru-Ptah, who died suddenly while her father was still alive. She was buried temporarily in her father's pyramid until her own tomb could be completed nearby, to which the whole burial was then transferred, leaving the sarcophagus behind. The new tomb remained intact, apart from water damage, until it was opened in 1956, yielding the princess's treasures.

The pyramid retains some of its ancient mysteries: once we observed three young village women climbing up the (now forbidden) path to the summit, each carrying one of the large mud-bricks from the pyramid on her head. At the top they danced slowly around in a circle, still with the bricks on their heads; then descended and disappeared. This little ritual was clearly some kind of supplication for fertlity to an ancient spirit associated with the pyramid, and it seems entirely possible that similar activities might occur at other ancient sites around the Fayoum.

The large, cratered area stretching away from the foot of the pyramid to the south and across to the other side of the modern canal is the site of the famed Labyrinth, of which there is little to see today: a few fragments of granite and limestone lotus columns litter the empty moonscape. But investigations carried out in 2008 by the National Research Institute of Astronomy and Geophysics using geophysical surveying techniques appear to support the suggestion that part of the Labyrinth lies yet to be discovered deeper below the surface than Petrie's and later excavations went. At the very least, "anomalies" and "linear features" have been revealed at depths up to 8 meters by such methods as very low frequency radio and ground penetrating radar.

The accepted theory until now has been that the Labyrinth was the mortuary temple of Amenemhat III, but because the apparent underground structures are out of alignment with the pyramid, scientists are now wondering if it may be older and served some other function. For a while we must wait: there is a plan first to drain the site of the very high level of ground water; then new excavations will tell us if what we thought had been quarried away is in fact lying beneath our feet.

Whether lost or hidden, the Labyrinth must have been an astounding building. Herodotus and Strabo were both lucky enough to visit it, and both described it in great wonder. Herodotus, who visited the Fayoum around the middle of the fifth century BCE writes:

> I visited this place and found it to surpass description; for if all the walls and other great works of the Greeks could be put together in one, they would not equal, either for labor or expense, this Labyrinth; and yet the temple of Ephesus is a building worthy of note, and so is the temple of Samos. The pyramids likewise surpass description, and are severally equal to a number of the greatest works of the Greeks, but the Labyrinth surpasses the pyramids. It has twelve courts, all of them roofed, with gates exactly opposite one another, six looking to the north end and six to the south. A single wall surrounds the entire building. There are two different sorts of chambers throughout–half underground, half above ground, the latter built upon the former; the whole number of these chambers is three thousand, fifteen hundred of each kind. The upper chambers I myself passed through and saw, and what I say concerning them is from my own observation; of the underground chambers I can only speak from report: for the keepers of the building could not be got to show them, since they contained (as they said) the sepulchres of the kings who built the Labyrinth, and also those of the sacred crocodiles. Thus it is from hearsay only that I can speak of the lower chambers. The upper chambers, however, I saw with my own eyes, and found them to excel all other human productions; for the passages through the houses, and the varied windings of the paths across the courts, excited in me infinite admiration, as I passed from the courts into the chambers, and from the chambers into colonnades, and from the colonnades into fresh houses, and again from these into courts unseen before. The roof was throughout of stone, like the walls; and the walls were carved all over with figures; every court was

surrounded with a colonnade, which was built of white stones, exquisitely fitted together.

'Labyrinth' is a Greek word that Brugsch says is derived from the Egyptian name of this Hawwâra temple, *elpa-rohunt*, 'temple of the mouth of the lake.' Reading Herodotus's description, it is easy to see how 'labyrinth' came to have its present meaning.

In the tombs around the pyramid, in 1888, Professor Petrie discovered the first of the famous Fayoum Portraits, the incredibly lifelike studies that were attached to the mummies of the deceased settlers of the Roman era in the Fayoum. Portraits were found in other parts of the Fayoum, and in other parts of Egypt, but most of those we now see in museums around the world were found here at Hawwâra. The pictures were mostly painted between 100 and 250 CE, and vary greatly in the quality of execution and preservation. They depict both men and women of all ages, as well as children, and among them Petrie believed he could discern a whole range of racial types: African, Greek, Macedonian, north Italian, south Italian, Moorish, Spaniard, Syrian, Indian; though he says the 'Egyptian type' rarely occurs. Many of the pictures are so skillfully executed that the modern observer can really believe in individual people full of character living two thousand years ago, rather than merely the faceless, floating names and mass generalizations of history books.

Petrie's studies showed that the portraits were painted during life, usually on a square piece of wood in melted, colored wax, and hung in the sitter's house. When the subject died, the portrait was sent along with the body to the embalmer, who roughly cut it down into an oblong with the top corners lopped off, to be positioned over the face of the mummy in the final wrapping. Petrie further deduced from the condition of the mummies and the rough manner in which they were buried that it was the tradition to keep the mummy of a deceased relative on public view in the atrium of the house for a generation or two, where it got knocked about, covered in dust, and damaged by occasional rain or in cleaning operations, until everyone eventually lost interest and it was taken away and carelessly buried, probably along with others from the same or a neighboring house, in an unmarked earth pit. It is the custom in the Fayoum today to keep photographs of the deceased of more than one generation on prominent display in the formal sitting-room of the family house.

The Kôm Ôshîm Museum now has one well-preserved mummy with portrait, and if you go to the Egyptian Museum in Cairo, make a special point of visiting Room 14, on the upper floor, where quite a large selection of the portraits is displayed. For superb reproductions of a great range of the portraits, as well as a very readable and enlightening text, see Euphrosyne Doxiadis's *The Mysterious Fayum Portraits*.

Lahûn Pyramid هرم اللاهون ▪ *haram al-lahûn*

Entrance fee. Take a service taxi from al-Ḥawâtim to al-Lahûn (1E3). The taxi usually stops at exactly the point where the route to the pyramid leaves the main road, and from here you must walk. It is a long walk (well over an hour), but a very pleasant one, provided the sun is not too hot. Follow the route described below for cars.

By private car, take the Beni Swêf road out of Fayoum, leaving the town in the south at al-Ḥawâtim. About 5 kilometers out of town, turn left at a main fork by a school. Follow the road until you reach al-Lahûn, 19 kilometers southeast of Fayoum, easily recognizable by the complicated array of canals, bridges, and sluices. Keep to the road as it twists around and crosses a modern iron bridge, then turn left down onto a dust track before the main road swings right again. On your left now is the old sluice bridge, built in the reign of Baybars I (1260–77). It was superseded in 1943, but for nearly seven hundred years before that time it had carefully regulated the amount of water entering the Fayoum.

At the first fork in the dust road, about level with the sluice bridge, bear right, then pass directly through the pretty village of al-Lahûn (bearing left at the main fork in the middle of the village) for about 1 kilometer, before reaching a T-junction at the end of the village. Turn left to attain an ancient embankment that leads you through the fields for several kilometers to the desert. Known now as Gisr Gadallah, this massive, twisting earthwork is thought to be part of the original barrage built by Amenemhat I in the Twelfth Dynasty (nineteenth to eighteenth centuries BCE) to divert water into the Fayoum as part of his project to enlarge Lake Moeris (see page 59). The masonry on the Nile Valley side of the embankment was added in the nineteenth century CE. Once you are out of the village onto the embankment, the pyramid becomes visible, a tall, irregular-shaped, dark lump rising quite dramatically out of the pale desert to the north, like some proud wart on a delicate skin.

The embankment finishes at the edge of the desert, and here is the ticket office and the security post. The pyramid was built over thirty-eight centuries ago, seven or eight centuries after the Great Pyramids of Gîza, by the architect Anupy for King Senwosret II, fourth king of the Twelfth Dynasty, grandfather of Amenemhat III. Senwosret reflected his family's special attachment to the Fayoum by choosing as the site of his eternal resting place a point overlooking the very entrance to the province—the 'Mouth of the Lake,' Le-hone, Lahûn. In fact, the site seems to have been chosen much more for its significant position than for its physical qualities as a base for such a massive structure. Petrie points out that Anupy must have been very concerned about possible subsidence of the soft brown marl on which the pyramid was partly built, as he fitted the outer casing of limestone into a socket at its base to prevent any outward movement, and then surrounded the pyramid with a trench filled with sand and covered with rolled flints. This was to function as a sponge in any occasional heavy rainstorm, when the volume of water running off the sides of the pyramid might otherwise be a danger to the marl base.

The pyramid was built on a natural mass of rock, partly cut away for emphasis. On this was placed a skeleton of massive limestone walls up to about half the height of the pyramid. The spaces between the walls were filled in with unburnt mud bricks, and the same bricks were used to build up the full height of the monument. Finally, an outer casing of limestone was placed over the bricks. But while Anupy could take measures to protect his pyramid against the once-in-a-lifetime ravages of the heavens, he could do nothing to protect it from human attack, and the outer casing is now entirely gone, the stone robbed at some stage for use elsewhere. The mud-brick core, subsequently exposed to the elements, has weathered into the dark lump we now see, and parts of the skeletal walls, also the object of stone-robbers' attentions until in view of the mud-brick mass above them it became too dangerous to work them further, can now be seen projecting from the body of the pyramid. With its skin eaten away, its flesh partly rotted, and its bones gnawed at, Lahûn is a sorry corpse of a pyramid, and yet it still imposes itself quite grandly on the scene and retains dignity.

Petrie entered the pyramid in 1920 and found the burial chamber empty apart from the granite sarcophagus, which was a plain work, but so accurately executed that the divergence from a straight line on each of its long sides was calculated at less than 0.005 of an inch. Although the chamber was empty, there had in fact been a royal burial, as proved by the gold uraeus from the king's crown found in the debris in one of the passages. The tomb had obviously been plundered, as had all the other royal tombs discovered here, including the small, hastily finished tomb number eight, at the bottom of a shaft south of the pyramid. Yet in tomb number eight in February 1914, Guy Brunton found something the thieves had missed, and made what in pre-Tutankhamun days was quite a spectacular discovery. In a block of mud in a recess that the thieves had ignored, Brunton discovered the jewelry of Princess Sat-Hathor-Int, who died in the time of Amenemhat III. The jewels, of very fine workmanship, include the feathered gold crown of the princess; over 1,300 tubular gold beads, thought to be decoration for a royal wig; necklaces; pectorals; silver mirrors; and many other pieces of gold, silver, carnelian, lazuli, and amethyst. The crown, half the gold beads, and a pectoral of Amenemhat III are now in the Egyptian Museum in Cairo, but the rest of the treasure left the country and is now in the Metropolitan Museum of Art in New York.

On the north side of the pyramid are eight rock-cut mastabas intended for royal use, but only one of them, the fifth from the west, was ever prepared for burial, and it is not even certain whether the burial took place. The shapeless mound east of the mastabas is the so-called Queen's Pyramid, but no tomb was found underneath it. Adjacent to the mastabas, a section of mud-brick wall interlined every four courses with rush matting is all that remains of the great enclosure wall, which originally encircled the pyramid at a height of up to ten meters.

East of the pyramid, at the edge of the cultivated land, Petrie excavated the valley temple and pyramid city of Kahun. Beyond these is the Coptic monastery of Dêr al-Ḥammâm.

Maydûm Pyramid هرم ميدوم ▪ *haram maydûm*

Entrance fee. Although not actually in the Fayoum, either geographically or politically, Maydûm pyramid is easily accessible and makes an interesting day-trip if you are based in Fayoum city.

Take an early train from Fayoum to al-Wâsṭa (4:30, 5:35 [ex. Fridays and holidays], 7:10, or 8:15), in the Nile Valley north of Beni Swêf. The hour's journey takes you first through the southeastern part of the Fayoum basin, then across the desert that separates the basin from the Nile Valley. For the last part of the journey, the pyramid, looking like a child's sandcastle on a beach in Brobdingnag, is visible on your left. At al-Wâsṭa take a service taxi to the village of Maydûm, a ten- or fifteen-minute ride. Alight at the far end of the village and walk the remaining short distance to the pyramid, first along a road through the fields and across two canals, then through the desert, carefully avoiding the skulls and bones of ancient burials, as well as the holes in which they once rested.

By car you can take the al-Wâsṭa road out of Fayoum, turning left at a T-junction in the desert just past the village of Demu. The road then leads through the desert, crossing the railway line, and comes to Maydûm pyramid before continuing to Maydûm village and al-Wâsṭa. The pyramid is also easily reached from the Cairo–Asyûṭ desert highway either directly from Cairo or from Fayoum via the Beni Swêf road. The turn east to the pyramid is 52 kilometers south along the highway from its beginning on the Cairo–Fayoum road, or 28 kilometers north along the highway from the junction with the Fayoum–Beni Swêf road.

The most attractive explanation of the strange shape of Maydûm pyramid, which is usually assigned to Sneferu (Fourth Dynasty), is provided by Kurt Mendelssohn in *The Riddle of the Pyramids:* Maydûm was one of the earliest attempts at pyramid-building, coming immediately after the very successful step pyramid of Saqqâra. It was built first as a small step pyramid, then enlarged, but before completion, plans were changed again and work was started to convert it into a 'true' pyramid by grafting on masonry from the bottom up, at an angle, to cover the steps. However, before this final stage could be completed, disaster struck when the whole outer casing, not being properly integrated into the structure of the pyramid, suddenly collapsed, resulting in the huge pile of rubble that now surrounds the base of the pyramid. The site was immediately abandoned, the mortuary temple remaining uncompleted, the stelae uninscribed, and the burial chamber unfinished, with the wooden props still in place. Meanwhile at Dahshûr, where the so-called Bent Pyramid was already half completed, plans were drastically revised as a direct result of the Maydûm disaster, and the angle of the building was cut for safety, giving this pyramid its distinctive 'bent' shape. Maydûm was never again used as a mortuary site. Others disagree with this scenario, citing a New Kingdom graffito in the mortuary temple that talks of "this beautiful monument"—an unlikely description if the pyramid had been in its current ruinous state at that time.

On the north side of the pyramid is the entrance to the burial chamber. The steep entrance gangway descends to the bottom of a well, from which you climb up into the burial chamber, where the walls are damp and you will soon feel the lack of oxygen.

Near the pyramid is an elongated, ruinous lump, which is the mastaba of Sneferu's courtiers. This is the source of the famous statues of Prince Rahotep and his wife Nofret and of the beautiful painted frieze of six geese feeding. Both are in Room 32 on the ground floor of the Egyptian Museum in Cairo.

Umm al-Atl أم الأثل ■ 'Place of the Tamarisk'

Umm al-Atl is the modern name for the ruins of the Ptolemaic village of Bacchias, on the northeastern edge of the Fayoum basin, not far from the larger town of Karanis (Kôm Ôshîm) (1E1). On the Cairo–Fayoum road, turn east at the bottom of the hill below the Kôm Ôshîm Museum onto a narrow tarmacked road that follows a canal along the edge of the cultivation. On your left at first are the ruins of Karanis, then the bare desert; on your right, the rich, green land drops away to the south. The gradient of the canal here is marked by the frequent weirs that punctuate its progress. These, along with the ducks and buffaloes that alike enjoy the rushing water, together with the timeless agricultural tableaux in the fields to the right, make this one of the Fayoum's more scenic routes. Some 11 kilometers from the junction, turn left over a bridge (there is a mosque with a very small minaret on the other side) and drive through the small village to reach the ruins of Umm al-Atl in the desert just beyond.

Bacchias, probably founded in the third century BCE and abandoned around the fourth century CE, contained some 700 houses, from which archaeologists estimate the population to have been around 3,000. The site has never been fully excavated, although an Italian team working here since 1993 has uncovered the stone structure of the village temple (dedicated to a form of Sobek, of course), which had previously been believed to be built entirely of mud brick—it is now thought that the large and solid mud-brick walls represent storerooms attached to the temple. The private houses of the village were of several stories, and the mud-brick walls of many still stand to nearly their original height, although they are mostly buried under sand and debris. The Italian team is in the process of clearing some of the houses, so you can now look inside almost complete upper-story rooms. It is intriguing to conjecture what may yet be discovered as excavations continue. Papyri and coins have already been recovered; both add substantially to the historical understanding of this site and others like it.

Sêla Pyramid هرم سيلا ▪ *haram sêla*

If you are feeling adventurous and energetic, you can go on from Umm al-Atl to the mysterious pyramid of Sêla, one of only seven 'layer monuments' in Egypt, which are not tombs and have few signs of religious ritual. Some experts suggest that these monuments were erected as regional symbols of the king's overarching power; certainly, Sêla pyramid commands a suitable position, sited on the highest point of the desert hills that separate the Fayoum from the Nile Valley, and in its pristine state it would have been visible from large areas of both. The pyramid is small, its core built in steps from locally quarried yellow limestone, though somewhat ruinous, and it is not clear whether its original shape was a step pyramid or a benben (a two-stepped, squat obelisk that represented the primeval hill). A fragment of statue and two stelae found in the vicinity in the early 1990s allowed the pyramid to be dated to the reign of Sneferu, first king of the Fourth Dynasty, in the early Old Kingdom. Sand-filled pits around the monument may have accommodated trees.

From Umm al-Atl, continue along the canalside road around the edge of the green land. At a T-junction, turn right (this is the Gerza road from the Nile Valley to the Fayoum), then immediately left and hook around to regain the road following the canal. From here, the road is unsurfaced and is bumpy, dusty, and narrow. If your vehicle will bear it, follow this road for 8 kilometers until you reach a bridge with a weir under it. Cross the bridge and follow the track around the fields and then left along the bottom of the cliffs to reach the *ghafîr*'s post near a sign announcing the pyramid. Leave your vehicle here, and the *ghafîr* will guide you through the desert and up the hills to the pyramid, which does not even become visible until you are almost upon it. The walk takes the best part of an hour and is demanding (wear a hat and carry water) but eventually rewarding: the views on a clear day are magnificent, and the mystique and sense of forgotten time of the pyramid are inspiring. There are fossil shells and petrified wood in the hills, and keep a lookout for birds: on my last visit, as we descended through a stinging and sometimes blinding sandstorm, through which the sun somehow also managed to burn, I saw an Egyptian vulture gliding and circling slowly above the edge of the fields. In modern convention, the Egyptian vulture is the first letter of the hieroglyphic alphabet, its *alif*–a beginning at the end.

Bibliography

Ahmed Zéki Bey. "Une description arabe du Fayoum au VIIe siècle de l'hégire." *Bulletin de la Société Khédivale de Géographie* vol. 5, 1898.

Ali Shafei Bey. "Fayoum Irrigation as described by Nabulsi in 1245 A.D." *Bulletin de la Société Royale de Géographie d'Egypte* vol. 20, 1940.

Baedeker, K. *Egypt, Handbook for Travellers*. London, 1878.

Baedeker, K. *Egypt, Handbook for Travellers*. Revised ed. London,1929.

Bagnall, R.S. and D.W. Rathbone, eds. *Egypt from Alexander to the Copts: An Archaeological and Historical Guide*. Cairo: The American University in Cairo Press, 2008.

Ball, J. *Contributions to the Geography of Egypt*. Cairo, 1938.

Bilainkin, G. *Cairo to Riyadh Diary*. London, 1950.

Brunton, G. *Lahun I: The Treasure*. London, 1920. *Cambridge Ancient History*, vol. 1, part 2. Cambridge: Cambridge University Press, 1971.

Capuani, Massimo, et al. *Christian Egypt: The Coptic Church through Two Millennia*. Edited and introduced by Gawdat Gabra. The Liturgical Press and the American University in Cairo Press, 2002.

Dehérain, H. *Histoire de la Nation Égyptienne*, vol. 5, 1931.

Description de l'Egypte. "Etat Moderne," t. 2 (1). Paris, 1812.

Doxiadis, Euphrosyne. *The Mysterious Fayum Portraits: Faces from Ancient Egypt*. London: Thames & Hudson, and Cairo: The American University in Cairo Press, 2000.

Encyclopedia of Islam. New ed. Leiden: E.J. Brill, 1960–.

Encyclopédie de l'Islam. 1881–1928.

Fraser, P. M. *Ptolemaic Alexandria*. Oxford: Clarendon Press, 1972.

Herodotus. *The History of Herodotus*. Trans: G. Rawlinson. London, 1862.

Holt, P. M., ed. *Political and Social Change in Modern Egypt: Historical Studies from the Ottoman conquest to the United Arab Republic.* Oxford: Oxford University Press, 1968.

Ibn Iyas. *Histoire des Mamelouks Circassiens.* Trans: G. Wiet. Publications de l'Institut Français d'Archéologie Orientale: Textes et Traductions d'auteurs orientaux, t.6. Cairo, 1945–.

Joannes, Bishop of Nikiou. *Chronique de Jean, Evêque de Nikiou.* Trans: M. H. Zotenberg. n.p., 1883.

Kees, H. *Ancient Egypt: A Cultural Topography.* Trans: I.D.F. Morrow. London: Faber and Faber, 1961.

Lane, E. W. *Description of Egypt.* Edited by Jason Thompson. Cairo: The American University in Cairo Press, 2000.

Lane, M. E. *Guide to the Antiquities of the Fayyum.* Cairo: The American University in Cairo Press, 1985.

Lane-Poole, S. *A History of Egypt in the Middle Ages.* London, 1901.

Lenoir, P. *Le Fayoum, le Sinai et Petra.* Paris, 1872.

Lucas, P. *Troisième Voyage, fait en 1714*, vol. 2. Rouen, 1719.

Mendelssohn, K. *The Riddle of the Pyramids.* London: Thames and Hudson, 1974.

Petrie, W. M. F. *Hawara, Biahmu and Arsinoë.* London, 1889.

——. *Roman Portraits and Memphis IV.* London, 1911.

—— et al. *Lahun II.* London, 1923.

Pococke, R. *A Description of the East*, vol. 1. London, 1743.

Salmon, G. "Répertoire géographique de la province du Fayoum, d'après le Kitab Tarikh al-Fayyoum d'an-Naboulsi." *Bulletin de l'Institut Français d'Archéologie Orientale* vol. 1, 1901.

Strabo. *The Geography of Strabo*, book 17. Trans. H. L. Jones. London, 1932.

Swelim, Nabil. "Seven Layer Monuments of the Early Old Kingdom." Lecture, Polish Archaeological Institute, Cairo, 19 June 2007.

"Traveling with Bedouin, Farmers and Fishermen: Ecotourism for Sustainable Development in the Fayoum Oasis." Feasibility study prepared for the [Egyptian] Tourism Development Authority and North South Consultants Exchange. [Cairo], 2000.

Index

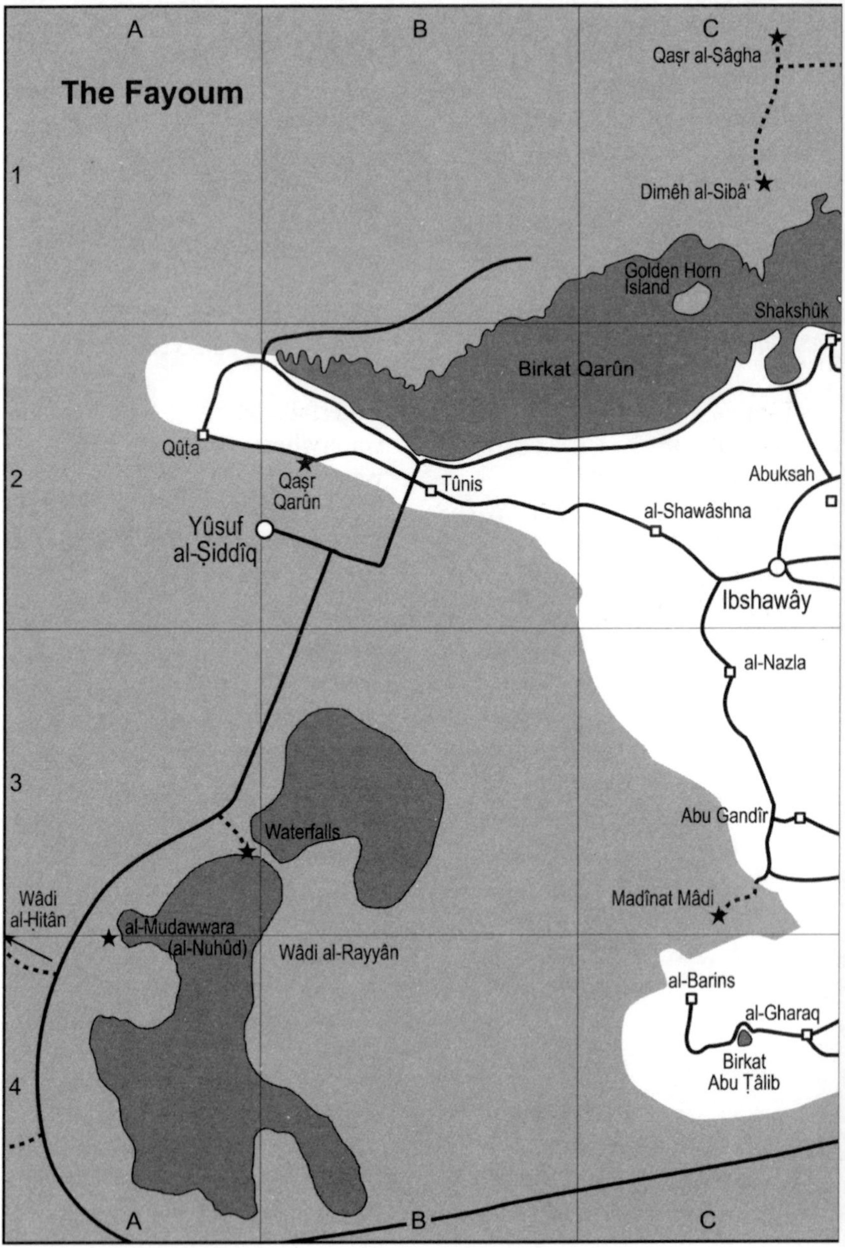
A
B
C
The Fayoum
1
2
3
4
Qaṣr al-Ṣâgha
Dimêh al-Sibâ'
Golden Horn Island
Shakshûk
Birkat Qarûn
Qûṭa
Qaṣr Qarûn
Tûnis
Abuksah
al-Shawâshna
Yûsuf al-Ṣiddîq
Ibshawây
al-Nazla
Abu Gandîr
Waterfalls
Madînat Mâdi
Wâdi al-Ḥitân
al-Mudawwara (al-Nuhûd)
Wâdi al-Rayyân
al-Barins
al-Gharaq
Birkat Abu Ṭâlib
A
B
C

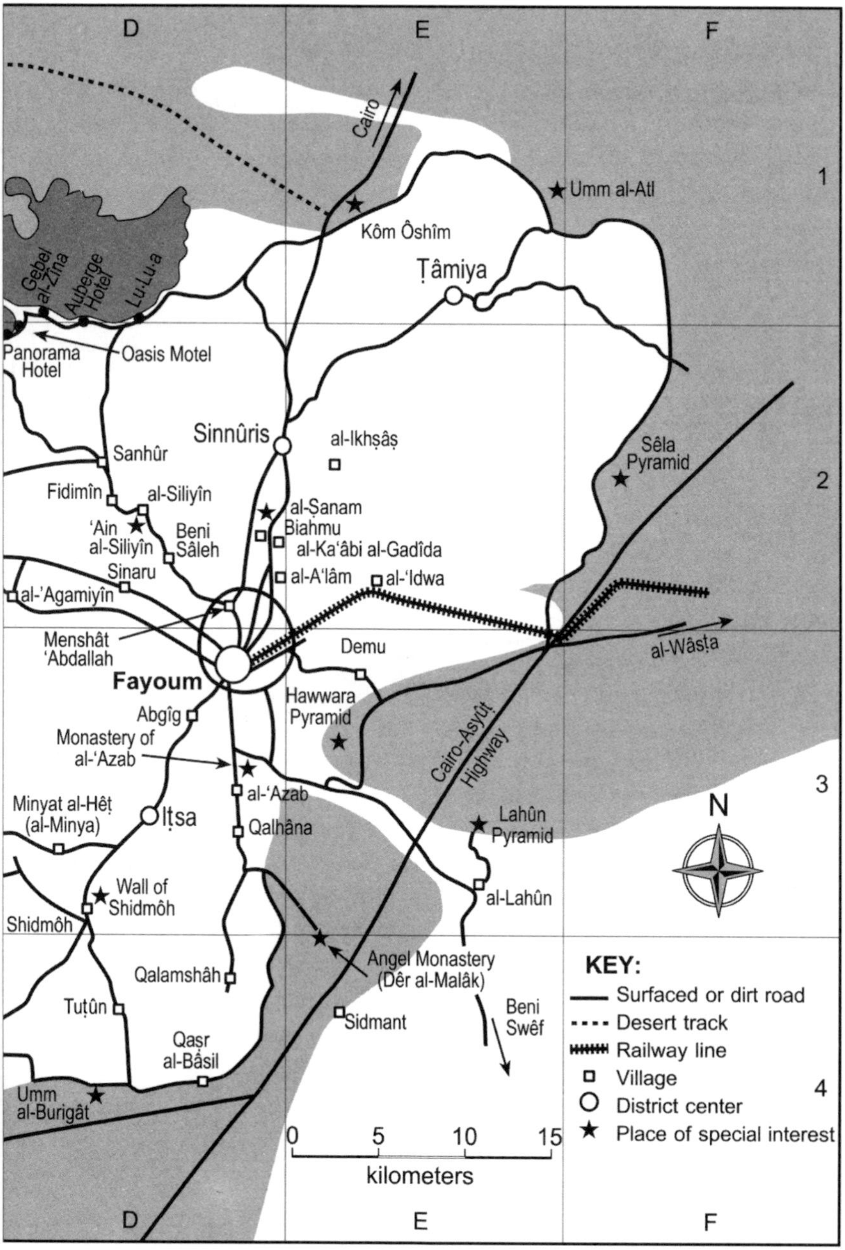
D
E
F
1
2
3
4
Cairo
Kôm Ôshîm
Umm al-Atl
Ṭâmiya
Gebel al-Zina
Auberge Hotel
Lu-Lu-a
Panorama Hotel
Oasis Motel
Sinnûris
al-Ikhṣâṣ
Sanhûr
Sêla Pyramid
Fidimîn
al-Siliyîn
'Ain al-Siliyîn
Beni Sâleh
al-Ṣanam
Biahmu
al-Ka'âbi al-Gadîda
Sinaru
al-A'lâm
al-'Idwa
al-'Agamiyîn
Menshât 'Abdallah
Demu
al-Wâsṭa
Fayoum
Hawwara Pyramid
Abgîg
Monastery of al-'Azab
Cairo-Asyûṭ Highway
al-'Azab
Minyat al-Hêṭ (al-Minya)
Iṭsa
Qalhâna
Lahûn Pyramid
N
Wall of Shidmôh
al-Lahûn
Shidmôh
Angel Monastery (Dêr al-Malâk)
Qalamshâh
Tuṭûn
Sidmant
Beni Swêf
Qasr al-Bâsil
Umm al-Burigât
0
5
10
15
kilometers
KEY:
Surfaced or dirt road
Desert track
Railway line
Village
District center
Place of special interest

Map 1

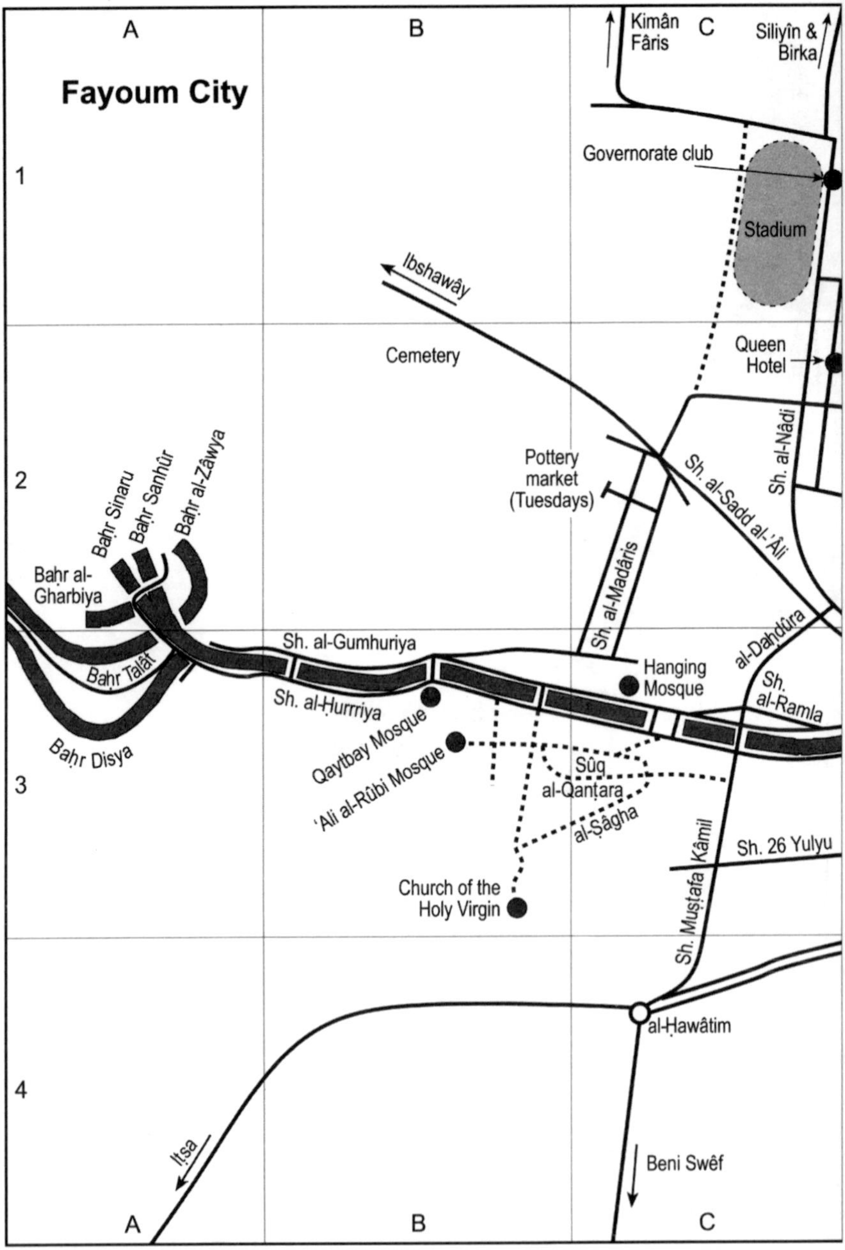
A
B
C
1
2
3
4
Fayoum City
Kimân Fâris
Siliyîn & Birka
Governorate club
Stadium
Ibshawây
Cemetery
Queen Hotel
Sh. al-Nâdi
Pottery market (Tuesdays)
Sh. al-Sadd al-'Âli
Sh. al-Madâris
Bahr Sinaru
Bahr Sanhûr
Bahr al-Zâwya
Bahr al-Gharbiya
Bahr Talât
Bahr Disya
Sh. al-Gumhuriya
Sh. al-Hurriya
Hanging Mosque
al-Dahdûra
Sh. al-Ramla
Qaytbay Mosque
'Ali al-Rûbi Mosque
Sûq al-Qantara
al-Sâgha
Sh. Mustafa Kâmil
Sh. 26 Yulyu
Church of the Holy Virgin
al-Hawâtim
Itsa
Beni Swêf

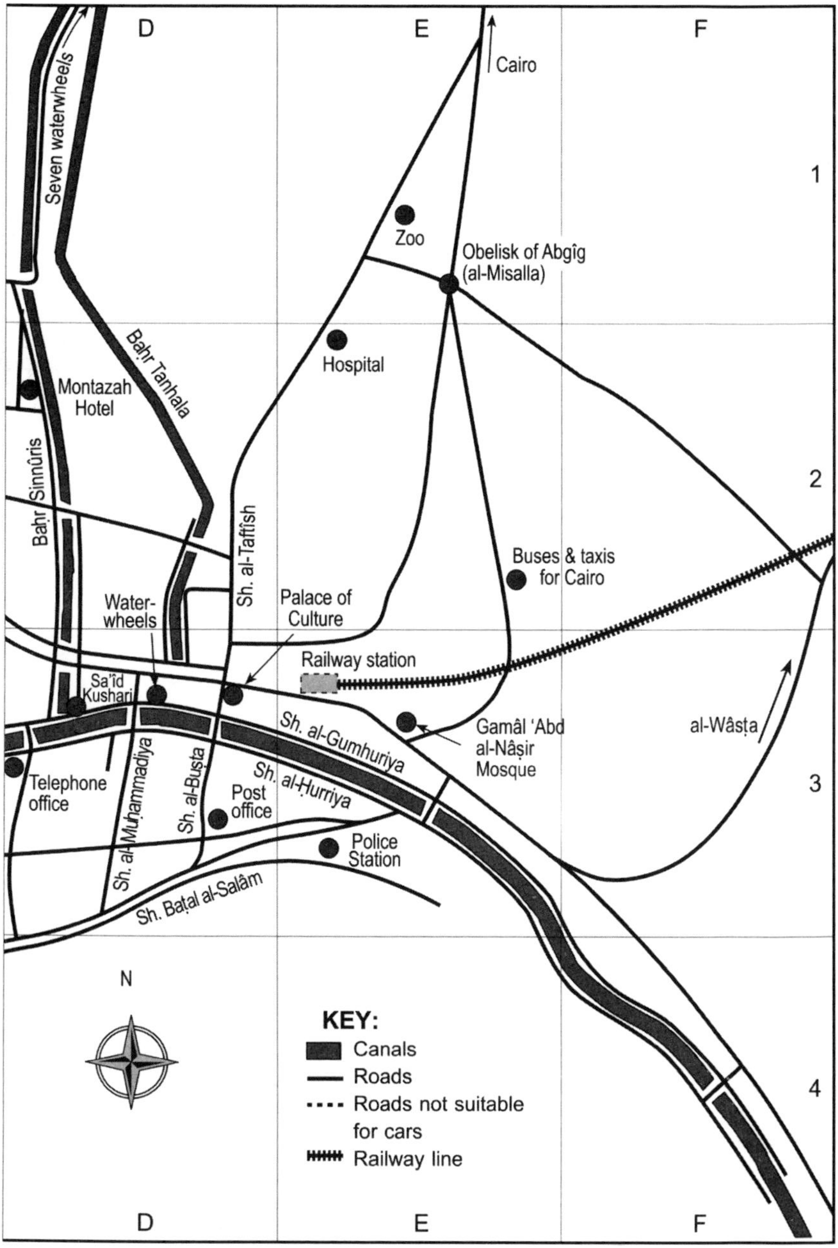
D
E
F
Cairo
1
Seven waterwheels
Zoo
Obelisk of Abgîg
(al-Misalla)
Hospital
Baḥr Tanhala
Montazah
Hotel
Bahr Sinnûris
2
Sh. al-Taftîsh
Buses & taxis
for Cairo
Water-
wheels
Palace of
Culture
Railway station
Sa'îd
Kushari
Sh. al-Gumhuriya
Gamâl 'Abd
al-Nâṣir
Mosque
al-Wâsṭa
Telephone
office
Sh. al-Muḥammadiya
Sh. al-Busṭa
Post
office
Sh. al-Ḥurriya
3
Police
Station
Sh. Baṭal al-Salâm
N
KEY:
Canals
Roads
Roads not suitable
for cars
Railway line
4
D
E
F

Map 2